THE PASCHATS AND THE CRYSTAL PEOPLE

THE
PASCHATS
AND THE
CRYSTAL
PEOPLE

Murry Hope

THOTH PUBLICATIONS

Thoth Publications
64 Leopold Street
Loughborough
LE11 5DN

ISBN 978 1 870450 13 3

Printed in the United Kingdom by Booksprint

To Patsy with my deepest gratitude and love

ACKNOWLEDGEMENTS

My gratitude and sincere thanks to Cynthia Kenyon for invaluable assistance with editing; to George Curzon for his scientific check and recommendations; to Dolores Ashcroft-Nowicki and her student Marten de Boer for the photograph and Museum details of the Hohlenstein-Stadel leonine figurine, to Dr. An Pang Tsai of the Institute for Materials Research, Tohoku University, Japan, for the excellent photograph of the quasi-crystal (originally reproduced in *Scientific American,* April 1991).

ACKNOWLEDGMENTS

CONTENTS

INTRODUCTION

The further one goes, the less one knows,
Therefore the sage knows without going about,
Understands without seeing,
And accomplishes without action.

Lao Tzu

When I was first encouraged to share my knowledge of the Paschats and the Crystal people with the world at large my former life as a 'closet alien' had to be dispensed with once and for all and the consequences of committing my beliefs to paper faced, endured and transmuted.

Since those times, however, I have been heartened by the response I have received from people in many parts of the world, which has helped to reassure me that, if I am the 'fool' that the dialectical materialist or the more rational amongst us might believe, then there are an awful lot of us about. But perhaps we may take comfort in the old adage 'when the world adopts the fool's beliefs, he is no longer the fool!'

As was the case with THE LION PEOPLE, the ensuing texts are the result of a joint effort between the Paschats Kaini and Mikili, their Crystal friends to whom my readers will be introduced in the forthcoming chapters and your author, who is little more than their translator, or mouthpiece if the contact has been a verbal one. One thing that must be made quite clear at this point is that I make no claim whatsoever to having the answers to everything, or being in any way a fount of cosmic knowledge, and this also applies to my Siriun friends. But it is felt that the latter may be able to pass on a little knowledge, and offer a few words of advice, that could help many people to cope with the inevitable evolutionary quantum leap that is destined to affect all life on Earth over the years that lie ahead in Earth time. Also, since it is the eventual destiny of mankind to negotiate both space and time travel, a few tips regarding the pros and cons of this future venture might not go amiss.

I must confess to being apprehensive when I first introduced the Paschats and their dedicated task to help humanity, but I need not have worried. Of the many, many people who have experienced them, either via *THE LION PEOPLE* as a book, or mystically within the space of their own consciousness, the one impression that has been almost universally received is that of overpowering love and understanding, and I have been greatly moved by the number of people who have effected their own contacts with Paschats, quite aside from my book and my dialogues with Kaini and Mikili and their clan.

One lady wrote to me of such a contact she had received when working with a fellow doctor as far back as 1944, which they felt they could not tell anyone for fear of ridicule.

Lion power is certainly taking off in a big way and your author cannot take all the credit – or is not entirely to blame, as the case may be – the Paschats and their Crystal friends having ensured that their words of light and wisdom are spread as evenly as possible over the spiritual gloom of this suffering planet. Nor has this shower of cosmic awareness been limited to shamanic, mediumistic or other mystical channels. Astrologers are observing that, as the balancing arm of the Aquarius/Leo axis, the leonine energies are essential to all life on Earth during the unfolding Age; giants of the scientific world such as Dr. Charles Muses *(The Lion Path)* are adding to its credulity, and a recent pamphlet that arrived on my desk from the World Ascension Network, which appears to be greatly concerned with the acknowledgement of the divine mother, and 'the balancing of the female flame within each of us', states:

> 'Our most significant approaching activation shall take place this year on August 8th (8:8)1991 and will be brought forth by a stargate known as THE LION'S GATE. This stargate has always been functional, and is the Giza/Egypt stargate previously mentioned. Throughout history the LION'S GATE has served as Earth's primary inter-dimensional doorway for energy exchange and initiation...'

This would appear to be confirmed in Hopi, Tibetan and Mayan sources.

My close associates and dear friends have often remarked on how privileged we are to have access to a little of the Paschat and Crystal knowledge; we could not possibly handle it in its entirety as our brains are not yet programmed to cope with the immensity and seeming complexity of its concepts; and yet we are assured that, once understood, the functions of the Universe are pure simplicity. It is only because of the mental convolutions that our own limited science has imposed upon us that we fail to distinguish the wood from the trees.

Readers with any degree of cosmic sensitivity will have no difficulty in noting the different quality of the Paschat and Crystal energies and, as a former member of the leonine clan, I have to confess that, for me anyway, the former make 'easier going' than the latter. The Crystal frequency inclines to the clinical and their message has a tendency to be somewhat stark and outspoken. The Paschats, on the other hand, have a warmth that many find endearing and although some critics of *THE LION PEOPLE* have seen fit to scoff at Kaini's 'dear things'mode of address, personally I feel it adds a warm, caring touch; but then I would, wouldn't I!

As many of the questions I am featuring have been put to both the Paschats and the Crystal people over a period of time, there is naturally a degree of repetition, people tending to pursue similar lines of enquiry. But rather than edit the answers, which each contain different slants or observations anyway, I have chosen to insert them in full and therefore crave the indulgence of my readers as far as this issue is concerned.

Since the final chapter of this book presents a degree of empirical evidence for some of the information given, plus the latest findings in certain fields of research that are applicable to our subject matter, my science editor has suggested that some readers, especially those unfamiliar with previous Paschat/Crystal material (see *The Lion People),* might find it easier to start with Chapter 12 and then return to the beginning.

Now comes the point at which I must hold my peace and let those better informed on such matters speak for themselves. Ladies and gentlemen, I hand you over to my beloved teachers, Kaini and Mikili, who will, in turn, introduce you to the Crystal people

Chapter 1

KAINI

INTERWOVEN UNIVERSES:

For those of my readers whose acquaintance I have not yet had the pleasure of making, may I introduce myself. You may call me Kaini, as this is the nearest approximation to my personal sonic in the sounds of your world. Likewise my female companion, who is both my equal and *my* complement, may be called Mikili. Mikili and I have both accepted different roles in respect of our dedication to the service of the peoples of Earth during the ensuing period *in your time*. Mine is more concerned with what you might categorize as cosmic knowledge, although I hasten to add that much of it *will* be, for the moment anyway, more metaphysical than physical. Mikili, on the other hand, concerns herself more with personal *issues* such as the psychology of the individual, healing and the assuagement of the suffering endured by the life forms on Earth caused by the cosmic virus to which your planet has been subjected for so many centuries; again I refer to your linear time. But, in all this, we are both, as are our Crystal friends, limited by the vocabulary and terms of reference available in the cerebral computer (brain) of our channel and her ability to draw on her own race-memories of her origin within our species. Some of this knowledge is, *of* course, locked in her genes, since it was known to former civilizations *that* existed in the pre-history of your planet but, for the most part, she is thrown back on her transpersonal frequencies which, as many of you who pursue the path of light, love and knowledge are well aware, are extremely difficult to access in the prevailing, suffocating climate of materialism in which your world is at present encloaked. So, dear things, do not expect perfection from any of us. We will do our best to present you with a picture that at the most will broaden your cosmic horizons and, at the least, may help *you* to effect your own transpersonal connections with their resultant realizations.

OUR UNIVERSE?

In my earlier teachings I spoke of time and *its* significance as far as the future of your planet is concerned. I described how we, the Paschats, a race of leonids from the binary star system you call Sirius or Sothis, once enjoyed the luxury of our own planet, which was eventually destroyed on the collapse of the smaller star, and how we were rescued by the Crystal people from the larger planet that orbited the blue-white star you now see in your night skies. I also explained how we were, in fact, *from your future* and looking back into both our own past and your present, which to us is also in the dead and distant past as far as your timing is concerned. Sounds complicated, does it not? But an understanding of the true nature and energy of time is something that your people will have to come to terms with sooner or later if you are to survive that which we are able to see for you as we look back from our future into your present and future.

In truth all time exists simultaneously. It is only separated by the limit of the frequency into which it *appears* to be encapsulated. As one of your more enlightened scientists once remarked, `Time exists in stationary bands through which we pass.' And, may I add, those stationary bands all exist concurrently so, although you may experience the effect of being bound within time at a given frequency, this is due to the limitations imposed by the evolutionary state of your cerebral programming. Since many of you, especially among the younger generation, are familiar with computer terminology, let me put it this way: the disks that effect your cerebral output need to be reprogrammed so as to engage a more comprehensive input, which would stimulate your neurones into circuits conducive to new degrees of awareness that could be automatically accepted by you as 'the norm'. After all, if you look back over the past hundred or so years of your history, you will observe that the technology of today might assume an almost magical quality if viewed by those living in, say, the year 1720. Or you could find yourself being dunked in the local pond for witchcraft were you to be observed switching on an electric light by anyone living in the reign of Elizabeth I. No?

So let us return to the different dimensions of time and the energies within those dimensions that propel matter through them. One question I am always being asked is: 'You say you are from the future and yet you speak of your own planet in the Siriun system. Is this planet still there and, if we were to fly there by rocket propulsion, would we find you all happily sitting around your sacred tree meditating?' The answer must, of course, be 'good gracious, no!' The Siriun system that housed our old domains is eight and a half light years away (by your reckoning), and this means that, by the time you see the blue star twinkling, all that time has passed between that 'twinkle' and your view of it. Take into account that according to your scientists' calculations light travels at approximately 186,000 miles per second and you will get some idea of the time difference, in terms of Earth years, that exists between our two worlds.

Of course, were you to take an extended journey by rocket propulsion to the vicinity of our star system – assuming that those travelling in such a primitive spaceship *actually lived long enough to make the journey,* which is highly doubtful even by your own calculations – you would find that the planets upon which we and the Crystal people once lived are no longer inhabited. And yet Sirius always has and will continue to exert a profound influence upon not only your solar system but the whole of a given portion of the galaxy for which it represents the central Sun or governing energy. This has been observed by many of your own researchers, especially those who have spent time delving into the mysteries of ancient Egypt. So, how is it done and how do we and our Crystal cousins manage to 'look in' on your present (which is our past) and present ourselves in the physical garbs of our past in which we would be more easily recognized by you at your present stage of somatic evolution and according to the standards accepted by your current understanding of physical science? Simple – we time travel!

Since all time is one, all one has to do is to discover the circuits of time, which interconnect all universes. Passing through some of these is no easy matter, however, since the frequencies involved are not conducive to the arrangement of certain particles and molecules that accord with your own physical universe. In simple language, your bodies would disintegrate and only if you possessed the knowledge of how to manipulate what are termed in your ancient teachings the *subtle bodies* could you survive. And yet there are really no such things as subtle bodies in the traditionally accepted understanding of the term since, once the evolving psyche has passed a certain point in its cosmic development, it can effect the adjustment *by will;* and therein lies the paradox!

There are many practices concerned with time travel that you will eventually learn, such as the adoption of a given `form' for the purpose of effecting a recognition with intelligences of alien appearance encountered during future journeys. Some of you might equate this process with what is referred to in metaphysical parlance as 'shape- shifting', although your present concept of this is limited to say the least. In actual fact we Paschats, like our Crystal cousins, are beings of pure energy, having long since discarded our furry bodies; and yet we choose to come to you in the form of the species through which we originally evolved because that is the one most comfortable for us to manifest in a material universe.

If you are thinking that all universes are not physical in the way that you conceive of that state, then you are perfectly correct. There are also parallel material universes, in which aspects of yourselves are simultaneously experiencing, as we explained in *THE LION PEOPLE.* So when you are feeling particularly low because, perhaps, the finances are in a bad state, the health is playing you up or your current romance has folded, consider that you may well be on an 'up' elsewhere in the universe. Taking the overall picture, things do have a habit of balancing themselves out.

We often watch those of you who group together for the purpose of meditation, healing, spiritual exploration or other cosmically worthy causes. We note how you send your thoughts out for this and that cause. Those thoughts, if properly organized, can represent a stream of conscious particle-wave packets that will accrete similarly charged particles, thus effecting changes at both the physical and subtle levels. Sadly, however, in many cases the input from each member of the group does not harmonize or match up, which causes a decrease in the energy potential of the thoughts sent out and a consequent blunting of the desired effect. It is always advisable to realize that in any group the energy frequency attained to is usually ordained by the least advanced, unless an incarnate 'cosmic' identity is present to control the proceedings.

And, while you sit in your little groups, reaching for those spiritual heights and the ecstasy so often associated with the mystical union of the higher and lower self, all the universes I have previously mentioned, plus innumerable worlds that I and my kind have yet to explore and understand, are also present. But which of those worlds you as an individual are able to look into will depend on your own personal stage of cosmic maturity, which is why, of course, you are often faced with the perplexing situation that you each receive different impressions or information! The same principle also applies to those among your so-termed 'rationalists' who supplement their incomes by assuming the role of professional debunkers. Even your own psychologists know about the 'experimenter effect', which means that whoever is conducting the experiment will affect the outcome according to his or her particular beliefs. Your physicists will tell you that minute particles, when observed, behave entirely differently than they are believed to do normally (which is, in fact, quite true) and will often reflect the observer in some way or other. But, take heart, dear things. The days of the debunker are numbered. We know because we have seen what is to come.

CONCERNING PROPHECY

'Then why don't you tell us, and put us out of our misery?' you may ask. The answer is: `Because we are strict observers of cosmic law we are not empowered to interfere with the evolutionary progression or retrogression of other species in other worlds or universes. And, since our universe functions at a frequency far removed from yours, any interference from or interplay between the two *prior to your entry into a given cosmic time-warp would* cause more suffering than you could possibly imagine. But enter that time warp you eventually will and the evolutionary quantum leap that is destined to catapult your planet into a new dimension, thus freeing it from the cosmic virus that has afflicted it and all that dwell upon its bosom for so many aeons, will herald the new golden age that so many of your mystics, psychics and pursuants of the path of light and love have envisioned for many centuries. Upon which note I will leave you to think about what questions you would like to ask me, before handing over to my dear Mikili.

QUESTION: This golden age you speak of seems to infer a drastic change in human nature. As a psychologist I am only too aware of how people tick and I have to confess that the kind of change of attitudes you imply does strain my credulity somewhat, although I would love to believe that you are right.

ANSWER: Your professional knowledge and experience must tell you that what you term 'human nature' cannot change overnight. Centuries of faulty programming will require a long period of deconditioning before the mind, via its cerebral computer, is able to effect the required transmutation and that will take time. But then time is an energy in itself and as such it both heals and transmutes, at all levels. It should also be borne in mind that there will be enormous physical changes to cope with in addition to the heightened frequency so, while the survivors are busy dealing with the former, the latter will be effecting its adjustments subtly via the subconscious. Those destined to survive the cataclysm *will have chosen the experience prior to birth,* anyway, so it will not come as such a shock to them when the time arrives. Besides, 'external' help will be at hand, initially anyway.

QUESTION: What did you mean when you referred to a 'cosmic identity' and how could such a being regulate the frequency or energy-level of a group?

ANSWER: In speaking of a 'cosmic identity' I am not referring to a discarnate being or 'guide' as you often call such communicators, but to someone incarnate in one of your Earth bodies who is not of your world, who is much time-travelled and who has brought through to the present some of the knowhow gathered during his or her inter-cosmic wanderings.

QUESTION: Are there a lot of such people around and from whereabouts in the universe do they come?

ANSWER: Contrary to what many of you might believe, there are very few cosmic identities incarnate in Earth bodies, for reasons I explained in *THE LION PEOPLE.* A Crystal beingness would be more comfortable in an Earth body than a Paschat, for example, and Dolphin identities are also able to negotiate the hominid experience as both are affiliated to the element of water. But I can think of many ETs who would be extremely uncomfortable in one of your bodies, due to incompatibilities between their native nervous/mental/ endocrine systems and your own. In such cases there would be no point in their coming to you, since they would not be capable of functioning to their full potential as teachers and helpers.

QUESTION: In *THE LION PEOPLE* you mentioned that the Paschats and Crystal people had been on Earth before, which was why the ancient Egyptians, for example, were able to reproduce effigies of lion beings so accurately. Some of us are still debating as to whether you actually came in bodies or purely as overshadowers. Can you solve this one for us, please?

ANSWER: Both the Paschat and Crystal races have visited your Earth in earlier times, for which purpose they assumed bodies that would render them recognizable to a species such as your own, which is accustomed to seeing an intelligence in particle rather than wave form (solid, rather than as manifestations of pure energy operating in non-locality). Our second star collapsed aeons ago according to your time-reckoning, and since then both our race and that of the Crystal people have ceased to exist. This is why we refer to our communications as coming from 'the future', meaning the future from your standpoint. There were two main visitations: the first was as described when one of our archaic space-ships made an unscheduled stop on your planet due to a failure in the time-circuitry systems. The second occurred when a small group of Paschats and Crystal people 'appeared' to monitor the effects of the adjustment resulting from the intensification of frequency caused by the evolutionary quantum leap that took place during a tilting of the Earth's axis, effecting drastic alterations in the topography of your planet's surface. Mountains rose where there had previously been plains, coastlines underwent radical alterations and sudden and vast climatic changes occurred that affected many lands.

QUESTION: But did you actually carry out genetic engineering, as some channelled sources suggest?

ANSWER: If you mean did we erect laboratories and submit the natives to suspect surgical procedures the answer must be a positive and definite NO. And yet there are those among you who carry the Crystal gene to this day and with that gene also goes the knowledge of the Paschats, so how did it get here? Your Professor Fred Hoyle is quite correct in his 'panspermia theory' in which he suggests that microorganisms throughout the universe do carry genetic factors such as the DNA with which you are now familiar. It should also be borne in mind that microorganisms can travel via time's circuitry. The particular microorganisms that arrived at the time the Crystal people and Paschats made their second visit to

Earth actually carried certain elements of the Crystal genetic code (not by accident, of course, but we will leave our Crystal friends to tell you about all that later), which the alien visitors helped a certain group of selected individuals to absorb and cope with before returning to their own time zone. This one incident gave rise to the worldwide legends of 'divine ancestors' and the couplings between mortals and immortals.

The coming of the Lion people always has and always will be associated with evolutionary quantum leaps and the cleansing action these can or should have on a planet. But once our work is complete and Gaia is cleansed of her virus, there will be no further need for our manifestation and those among you who feel a closeness with us will once again return to their own. The Crystal influence will lead in the next age, the power of the lion transferring to the fabled unicorn (your planet's true symbol which Gaia inherited from her Crystal ancestors) just as your myth tells you.

One small tip concerning visits of friendly aliens to strange planets: there are only two stages in the evolution of a planet, including all life forms dwelling thereon, when this is possible: extreme primitivity, because any species with a potential for what you would recognize as intelligence would consider anything arriving from 'the heavens' or 'the spirit world' as supernatural, divine and therefore to be treated with great respect; and when a planet and its denizens are sufficiently advanced scientifically to understand fully the technology of the visitors, sensitive enough to be aware of their true intent and wise enough to return love and respect when it is duly accorded. I am sorry to have to inform you that ninety-nine point nine-nine-nine percent of claimed UFO sitings are not extra-terrestrials at all (either benign or malign!), but manifestations of errant energies emitted from your own planet, plus the intrusion of – oh dear, I am being told that I must leave that one for our Crystal cousins to explain as it falls more into their territory than ours.

Incidentally, anyone who has a memory of or feeling for Sirius, or any other extraterrestrial location, or even some prehistoric civilization on your own planet, the existence of which is still denied by your historians, does so because they carry that knowledge in their genetic memory-bank. They may not always be able to rationalize this and, in times past before the inter-space theme assumed its present popularity among certain sections of your society, such memories were associated with 'paradise', 'heaven', the Elysian fields and so forth, according to the prevailing religious emphasis. People without such genetic memories often experience extreme difficulty in accepting the beliefs of those who have them.

QUESTION: Could you tell us more about this virus that is afflicting Earth. Has it anything to do with what our scriptures call 'the fall'?

ANSWER: To answer the latter part of your question first, the answer is yes. Cosmic viruses are no more uncommon than are the viruses that attack your bodies from time to time. They carry a chaotic energy potential which will afflict the person, or planet as the case may be, since your planet is also a 'person' in the sense that she is a self-regulating entity with a lot more knowledge and foresight than your Professor Lovelock credits her with! Any carrier of a chaotic energy-potential is, by nature, destructive and in the case of a planet such as Earth, or Gaia as some of you prefer to call her, such a source of chaotic energy will wreak havoc in whichever field is weakest in both the host and those other life forms it sustains. Thus, when you suffer from a virus and are consequently unwell, all the other life forms on your body, many of which you cannot see and yet your medical scientists will tell you they are there, also suffer likewise. And if you have a particular weakness, then that will be the very area to which the offending virus will make. Since this question takes us right into Mikili's territory, I am now going to hand over to her to fill you in on what actually happened in those far-off times and how it is still affecting you to this very day.

Chapter 2

MIKILI AND KAINI

MIKILI:

THE 'FALL':

My dear ones, I welcome this opportunity to speak with you of things that affect each of you directly, because it is with such matters I am mostly concerned rather than with the whole picture, which is Kaini's province of instruction. Now the one event that took place during the early days of your planet's evolution was its invasion by an alien cosmic virus. If you care to refer to our previous teachings on the subject of good and evil, you will note that we defined what you term 'evil' as misplaced or misdirected energy that is out of its correct time-sequence. We also directed you to consider that there are many forms of evil and to simplify it in this way might well give you the idea that we are denying its existence, which is far from true. Of course evil exists, but only as relevant to time. Which brings me to comment on the question of dualism, or what is viewed by many of your beliefs as the continual battle between chaos and order, exemplified in your religious systems both old and new.

Chaos is part of the natural development of universes in that it is the dissolving factor as far as certain frequencies of physical matter are concerned. The particles that eventually come together to form whole universes emanated from those subatomic regions you might view as being chaotic. But seen from afar, or should I say outer time, they display a splendid symmetry that informs the viewer of the future pattern of their creation. It is only when one is close to their chaotic state that they exhibit a disturbing influence, in that they *apparently* fail to conform to those physical laws that are essentially associated with order and what is currently accepted as time's forward directional arrow. So, having established that the element of chaos is a natural manifestation of the continual change taking place in all universes, and individuals for that matter, let us return to our chaotic (out of its correct time sequence) virus and the havoc it appears to have wreaked on your lives and those of your ancestors.

When did it first afflict your Earth and whence did it come? I have heard it said that Sirius was the culprit, but this is not strictly true. I use the term 'strictly' because it did pass through the Sirius system, but the frequencies therein were much too fast for it on the one hand and totally incompatible to its manifestation on the other, so it was duly ejected. However, Sirius, being the `central Sun' for this part of the galaxy, emits a constant stream of energy which radiates through those celestial regions laid to its care, including your own solar system. But were this energy to reach you in its raw state, it would be more than your bodies, or psyches for that matter, could endure, so it is filtered down by being passed through a series of 'gates' if you care to think of them as such, in much the way that you use a transformer to adapt a powerful electric current for use in a small appliance. The first port of call for the Siriun energies destined for your neck of the cosmic woods is the constellation of Orion (in the celestial equator near Gemini and Taurus, containing the stars Betelgeuse and Rigel) from which it is then passed to Earth via your outer planets and finally to your Sun. Millions of years ago, by your reckoning, the offending cosmic virus, having been ejected from the Sirius system, infiltrated the transmission of energies from Sirius to the Orion area where it soon became drawn in.

Now it so happened that certain of the entities that inhabited the regions of those particular stars at the time were neither highly evolved, nor were their energies compatible with what was destined to be the hominid experience. As a result, they inevitably fell victim to the virus and, when the Siriun energies were passed on from the Orion constellation to your solar system, the illness was included with the 'package'.

Think of it this way: one of your computers regularly passes faxed messages for a major company to the satisfaction of all concerned. But, one day, some joker plants a computer virus in the system for some reason best known to him or herself. From then on the messages come through just the same, but with a slight distortion and it could be weeks, or even months, before the virus is identified and dealt with. Convert this into cosmic time and you have your picture!

When the virus first hit your solar system, most of the governing planetary cosmic intelligences were able to cope with it, such life-forms as their orbs sustained being incompatible with its manifestation in much the same way that a flower does not catch a headcold or a tree go down with a gastric ulcer. But the orb you now see as your Moon, which in the earlier days of its lifecycle did sustain a life-form through which the virus could manifest, became badly infected and slowly the infection was filtered down to your Earth. The illness entered its worst stage during the last axis tilt, when your planet moved slightly away from its parent Sun and in closer proximity to its Moon.

Since Siriun energies are essentially concerned with the cosmic principles of polarity and equilibrium, one of the main distortions caused by the virus has manifested on your planet as a polarity imbalance that has been the cause of suffering among your peoples for centuries. This imbalance has taken the form of over-emphasizing the animus (to use the term so aptly qualified by your great psychiatrist Carl Jung who, incidentally, carried the Crystal gene) in the male of your species and the anima in the female, whereas, were your polarity balances to be correctly adjusted, each would partake of both in equal measure. This has had several disastrous psychological effects on your people:

1. It has caused the male to seek his anima in the female and the female to seek her animus in the male and, since this seldom works out, emotional chaos frequently ensues. Some among you have already become aware that there is something wrong in this area of your psychology, but attempts to correct it at the general level have met with little if any success and the 'battle of the sexes' continues to rage. You have a saying 'being vegetarian is of no benefit to the sheep while the fox remains a carnivore'; well, the same applies to this particular problem which you are facing on your planet. The voices of the few will not be heard over those of the majority, until the minds of the majority are cleansed of the effects of the offending cosmic virus.

2. This over-emphasis of the animus has also given rise to a constant urge for belligerence, which may manifest in many different ways, ranging from outright war to vicious verbal debates and attitudes of rebellion/subjugation, that are often erroneously viewed as 'essential to growth'; also the over-emphasized need to compensate.

26

3. Since there are four further principles involved, about which our Crystal cousins will tell you more later, several other symptoms of this cosmic illness have manifested in the Earth hominid species. These include fear (as opposed to caution), spiritual and cosmic blindness, the unnatural and spiritually damaging separation between psyche and soma (or the essence-fragment and its physical vehicle as we prefer to say) and hominid egotism/speciesism/cosmic racism. As a species, my dear ones, you are no greater than any of Gaia's other children. Agreed, you might display what you see as intelligence, but there are other, more subtle levels of knowledge than the obvious ability to do your sums, make weapons of destruction and build ugly edifices in which to cram yourselves in the cause of 'civilization'. Besides, knowledge and wisdom are not necessarily synonymous. Hominids, like all Gaia's children, should enjoy the fresh air and unpolluted waters and feast their eyes on the profusion of plant and animal life which abounds on your once beautiful planet. I say 'once beautiful' because you have destroyed so much of it, not only with your actions, but also with your thoughts.

I call your attention to your biblical story of Adam and Eve which actually contains a grain of cosmic truth in that the 'knowledge' referred to (which incidentally, had nothing whatsoever to do with a serpent) was concerned with the anima/animus imbalance that has resulted in extreme suffering, particularly for the female of your species, ever since. Did you know, for example, that your breeding habits are completely out of gear? These should be regulated by a solar cycle, which would bring the female into a state of fertility once a year only, while also exerting a sobering influence on the over-emphasized libidos and aggressive tendencies in many of your males (and some of your females, come to that!). You can thank your Moon for your present state of affairs for it is indeed the friend of the male and not of the female as is popularly believed.

Should some of you think the correction of this imbalance would constitute a dampener on your 'fun', then I must tell you that you will not be around to enjoy the fruits of the bosom of Gaia after she has been helped to adjust her frequency to the level compatible with her true stage of cosmic development. In the forthcoming years of your Earth time there will be no place for cruelty, insensitivity, or any of the other symptoms of the offending viral illness; and those essence-fragments who have been subjected to these imbalances will need to return to other cosmic nurseries for cleansing and rehabilitation. Harsh words, but true, I fear. Your Earth is destined to enter another golden age, where the lion will lie with the lamb, the battle between males and females will cease because each will accord the other the respect he or she deserves and mankind will awaken to the realization of its planetary host and its true place in the cosmic scheme of things.

THE CURE:

The aforegoing naturally gives rise to many questions such as:

How can Gaia and her progeny be cured of this sickness to which all lifeforms on this your planet are exposed?

Are some immune to it and if so who?

What kind of measures are required to rid Gaia of the virus; must these be physical or can the healing be achieved by purely mental or metaphysical means?

The Siriun forces of light have sent their own missionaries, along with enlightened beings from other parts of the galaxy, to your Earth from time to time in the hope that mankind will accept their message and reject the illness itself via a process of mass self-healing for both the individual and the planet. But their messages of love, peace, caring and spiritual enlightenment have been rejected, or later twisted to suit either the whims of egotistical priests and gurus, or power hungry individuals who worship at the shrine of the gods of materialism. Sadly, because of the enforced separation of body and psyche (spirit) which has been a side-effect of the spiritual blindness caused by the virus, most people have either tended to take the easy way out and accept blindly the dogmas that have arisen from the misinterpretation of the myths of certain ancient races, or selected the cosy path of materialism which they feel to be the only substantial alternative.

So more stringent measures are now called for and 'cosmic physicians' are being called in to help Gaia eject her virus. In other words, violent upheavals on the surface of the Earth will constitute part of the evolutionary quantum leap that will take Gaia into a higher frequency which the virus cannot tolerate. Unfortunately, many of the hominids living on her surface will not be able to tolerate it either.

As to the question of immunity, of course there are people on Earth who have not fallen victim to this cosmic malaise. Your planet sustains a very broad spectrum of evolutionary stages, ranging from very young souls (I prefer the term 'cosmically immature essence-fragments') to those advanced beings who are gifted with the love and light generated by the impulses of genuine cosmic awareness. The great majority of humanity, unfortunately, lie somewhere in between these two poles, unable to make up their mind in which direction to move. It will be when Gaia finally shows her real strength that, to quote your scriptures, 'the goats will be separated from the lambs' and that separation will be self effected and NOT the work of some omnipotent deity sitting in judgement over you all. Mature fragments naturally recognize the viral symptoms, from which they are protected by being in closer contact with the higher frequencies emitted from their essences (transpersonal or higher selves as some of you prefer to say). Essence-fragments that are in the process of reaching spiritual maturation in this present time-zone (life), unlike their cosmically older brothers and sisters, will not have been born with this knowledge, but will develop it as they proceed through life. Those amongst you who come to spiritual realization and cosmic awareness later in life often fall into this category and the very act of seeking beyond the 'self will help you to cleanse yourselves of the illness we have discussed above.

When will all this take place? The exact dates are as yet unfixed in your time, since they will be governed by your own thoughts and actions. There was a point at which a great spiritual and mental effort on behalf of all humanity could have turned the tide and avoided the tragedy; sadly that has passed. But, mercifully, many of those among you who are now of the older generation will be spared the horror that is to come, although they may well return to help build that brave new world that mystics, visionaries and the spiritually motivated among you have dreamed of over the centuries. If all this sounds horrifying, then I am sorry. But is it not better to be prepared? I think I have said enough on this subject, so let us turn our attention to less disturbing thoughts.

ARCHETYPAL ROLES AND THE HEALING PROCESS:

As those of you who have read *THE LION PEOPLE* will know, my specific interest as far as your planet is concerned is healing – healing of all species and things. What do I mean by 'things', some of you may ask. You, my dear ones, are not the only intelligences experiencing through the various frequencies of matter that are manifest on your planet. Did you know, for example, that a piece of coal, a chair, a rose bush or even your motor car have an identity? Your ancients, who were motivated more by instinct than logic, were perfectly aware of all this, which is why they accorded certain objects special reverence; for it must be understood that because a 'thing' carries an intelligence quotient that may well be way below your own, *according to your standards,* it does not mean that it is necessarily chaotic by nature. Besides, there is such a thing as incompatibility. For example, you can have a nice motor car in which you feel really comfortable and enjoy driving and another that seems to play you up from the moment you sit inside it, whereas another driver might find the reverse. And the same applies to all 'things'. There are those with which some of you may feel distinctly uncomfortable, but which your friends may feel completely at home with. The fact that something does not accord with your personal frequencies should not necessarily be taken as an indication that it is malevolent, or out of its correct timesequence. But on the other hand it might be. If you are in doubt as to what I am talking about here, I refer you to a book by one of your own scientists, *THE NATURE OF THINGS* by Dr. Lyall Watson.

Coming back to the healing question, what I am trying to say is that you are not the only beings or intelligences living off Gaia that are in need of healing. The viral imbalance is general throughout your Earth. So, when you send out your healing thoughts, do spare a wee one for those appliances that are not working properly, the flower in your pot that has wilted for no apparent reason and the spirits of water that are trying so hard to combat pollution and drought. Were you to talk to (verbally acknowledge) the life force in every-thing, believe you me you would receive far more cooperation from 'things' all round.

Healing, as you know, can take many forms. In some of your countries, alternative therapists are allowed to work side by side with more orthodox practitioners of medicine. Of course, there will always be a need for doctors; or will there? You see, the process of self-healing, once it is understood and mastered, can in itself be used as a preventative, and that means being able to evade those circumstances that could give rise to, say, a traffic accident. If this sounds far-fetched let me hasten to assure you that in other worlds this has been achieved and the benefits reaped have left the inhabitants free to pursue other lines of study and enquiry. Of course, one is always learning and as soon as one lesson is mastered one is confronted by yet another and so forth. As we explained in *THE LION PEOPLE*, the tensions caused by the evolutionary thrust of the essence and its fragments exist in a degree appropriate to each time-zone. These tensions are part of the natural process of the universe and without them, whatever form they may take, you would have nothing to push against. There is, however, a vast difference between the natural forward motion of spiritual evolution and the extreme competitiveness to which your peoples are prone, which represents an overstatement of a natural principle.

But I must not get ahead of myself, or you for that matter, so let us give some thought to the question of the use of archetypes in the process of self-healing. All living things – and that means everything – respond to one or more archetypal principle. These archetypes vary in each time-zone according to the nature of the learning experiences afforded therein. As disease literally means dis-ease, or not being at ease with your true self and your surroundings, it is a help for you to know what your essence has chosen for the expression of its fragment (psyche) in its present life.

Your planet functions according to the numerical frequency of the number 12 plus one, as shown mathematically in the rhombic dodecahedron. There are (believe it or not) twelve planets in your solar system and twelve different archetypes are able to find form and expression through the experiences offered by life on Earth. The number 4 (and multiples thereof), as representing the basic elements through which life on your planet manifests, is also significant to you, especially at the material level. This is not necessarily so in other parts of the universe. Some places function on the number 8, 9, or even 15, which means that in the latter case, for example, the planet or level in question offers experience to 15 different archetypes. On some planets, there are advanced life-forms with the power of personal flight; on others, the incarnate fragments are able to live both within and above the waters. Equally, here on Earth you can undergo experiences that are denied in an '8' system, or any system based on a number under 12. A '15' system, on the other hand, may offer a greater variety while at the same time incorporating some of what you have to offer.

On Earth there are actually thirteen different forms of archetypal expression. For simplicity I have given them names to which you can relate:

Protector, teacher, artist, priest, server, ruler, scientist, parent, fool, collector, performer, child and time lord.

How these archetypes are expressed will depend on three factors:
1. The general conditions into which the essence-fragment or psyche incarnates.
2. Its own personal stage of cosmic maturity.
3. The overall development of the cosmic impulse or group soul in which it originated.

Thus a protector essence-fragment incarnating into primitive conditions could become an aggressor, soldier or mercenary, while in more civilized surroundings that psyche would express itself as a servant of the law, upholder of justice or military protector, which office it would carry out justly or otherwise according to its stage of spiritual maturity. It is possible, however, that should the group soul as an entity lag behind in its evolution, this can also affect those of its members who have progressed, who may conse-quently be held back or frustrated as a result. You see, being in incarnation is not just a question of you as an individual doing your thing as and when you want; you are also part of a group plan. And should some member of that group fail to fulfil a karma towards you that might, let us say, enable you to go to university, travel to another land in which you would be happier and more secure or fulfil yourself in some other meaningful way, the resulting spiritual and psychological frustration could prove highly injurious to your health and might even result in a terminal illness; likewise your duty to others, in which case that which you have caused them to suffer as a result of your neglect to fulfil a karma could also rebound on you.

When a person tries to act out a role in life that is alien to either his or her cosmic impulse (group soul) or basic essence, of which the incarnating psyche is but one fragment, an inversion of energies takes place so that the natural archetypal expression is forced inwards, there being no avenue through which it can express itself.

This is also disease-inducing, different diseases resulting from different archetypal malfunctions. This is why it is so important for the individual to discover his or her true self and not be misled into trying to fit into a role deemed suitable by society but unfulfilling to the archetype. For example, if you are pursuing the role of actor or actress because you enjoy the plaudits of the public, when you should be studying nursing or child care, no matter how much success you achieve you will always feel dissatisfied and 'out of gear'. Eventually some illness of a mental or psychosomatic origin will ensue and the general public inevitably asks why such a person, with so much money and such a lot going for them, should suffer so.

False archetypal roles are sometimes assumed by psyches for some special reason. Child archetypes may elect to enter a body in which they will be able to remain always the child, never accepting personal social responsibility. Or they may choose to incarnate into a body which has genetic deficiencies which, although it may cause them much personal frustration, could serve as a lesson to the parents to remind them that they are out of alignment with their group soul, and should be pursuing the role of caring for others instead of some more socially viable path.

Psyches resonating to one of the more academic or artistic archetypes, if forced into heavy labour or conditions that are not conducive to the expression of that impulse, will inevitably break down either physically or mentally, as will the more energetic-types who are forced to sit behind a desk, or study volumes of detail when they would be better employed in the great outdoors or in some more physical form of expression. As your own psychologists have observed, different diseases afflict different psychological types, and any among you who have worked with, say, terminal cancer patients, migraine sufferers, or those beset by diseases of the joints, will be able to observe a definite psychological pattern. Unfortunately, the demands imposed by modem society are hardly conducive to the discovery of the natural archetype and many of the illnesses experienced among the so-termed 'civilized' nations of your world are the result of square pegs being forced into round holes.

Another example would be a teacher, priest, or scientist in female incarnation who, if forced into the maternal mode, will experience deep frustration, while her more maternal sister, whose long working hours in a factory, office or laboratory deny her the experience of childbearing and home-making, will suffer likewise.

I have heard some of your counsellors telling their clients, 'You are obviously on the wrong path in life because if you had discovered your true purpose everything would go right for you.' To use one of your expressions of disbelief – 'balderdash'. It is by no means as simple as that. Besides, adopting such a simplistic attitude towards the woes of others is hardly constructive counselling. Nor does it say much for those great spiritual leaders and teachers who have suffered persecution and torture for their efforts. But maybe this thought has evaded some of you who have chosen the counselling path: or perhaps you yourselves would be better suited to the profession of artist, actor, protector or performer rather than server or teacher?

For those among you who may wish to know which of the archetypes I have named carry specific healing energies, let me explain that healing can take many forms. For example, music can heal, so therefore the performing musician or singer has a role to play; the scientist can also contribute towards the healing process via sane technology and a study of the physical laws; many of your medical doctors and specialists come within this archetype. The priest can heal by engendering spiritual understanding, while the fool brings laughter that dismisses depression and raises hopes and the teacher conveys self-healing techniques to those ready to handle them. But among the nurses, social workers, counsellors and the majority of those who have devoted their lives to healing, be it spiritual, psychological or physical, the server archetype predominates.

QUESTION: Could you please explain some of the archetypes you have mentioned that we do not understand. Collector, performer and time lord, for example?

Perhaps 'recorder' might be a better name for the collector, since, aside from the obvious, the collector archetype incorporates all those who are associated with aspects of your Earth's past: historians, mythologists, anthropologists, geologists, palaeontologists. To this group soul falls the keeping of all the records associated with your planet in general and your own species in particular. Such interests are not confined to the academic field, however; there are just as many keen amateurs, if not more. Also, there are numerous voluntary organizations that seek to keep alive some period from your historic past. Such people will delight in spending their weekends dressed up as Roman legionaries, roundheads or cavaliers, or groups from equivalent periods of historical relevance to each country. In other words, they keep the past alive by 'collecting and storing' history in one form or another.

Performers are by no means limited to the theatrical and allied professions. The political scene is swarming with them and every organization or gathering, from the parliaments and governing bodies of the various nations to the members of your local council, or women's institute, can usually come up with several who often delight in jockeying for position. Performers have their place, however. Being great organizers they are usually the promoters of action, even if they do not actually take part in this themselves. Their archetype is essential to the continual motion necessary to avoid stagnation.

Time lords are rare, but they nevertheless exist. The representatives of this cosmic impulse or group soul are few and far between on your planet, due to Earth being somewhat behind where it should be at its present stage of evolution. Your Albert Einstein was a time lord rather than a scientist (in my archetypal meaning of the word) and there are a few scientists and metaphysicians among you whose work may not be appreciated during their lifetime because they are 'ahead of their time'. But in years to come the wisdom of their conjectures will become obvious, just as it has taken your space explorations to prove the validity of earlier scientific theories such as time dilation and the space-time curve. All time lords are not scientists, however, nor are they all 'lords' in the masculine meaning of the word. There are also time ladies, if you see what I mean.

QUESTION: What would be the ideal lifestyle for people here on Earth and, were we to rid ourselves of the virus you mentioned earlier, would we then be able to live balanced, harmonious and caring lives?

ANSWER: The kind of chaos that faces many of you who are experiencing Earth lives need not be so. Yes, it would be possible for you to live in a more caring, loving, harmonious and balanced way. In fact you could do it now if you all pulled together, but the enormous range of soul-ages among you denies you the chance, since immature psyches, like young children, tend to be noisy, somewhat aggressive at times and highly egocentric.

The ideal life for Earthlings would be in small communities, in which each person has a place and purpose and knows from very early days which way he or she is going in life. Today, so many of you are totally lost; you do not know what to do with your lives, so you waste valuable time and energy that could be put to more constructive uses in the betterment of both your own circumstances and those of the community at large. Self-healing will eventually be taught in schools, as will such right-brain activities as telepathic communication with the other life forms with which you share your planet, the plants, trees, animals and elemental forces, for example.

QUESTION: Will we ever find a cure for cancer, or AIDS, for that matter?

ANSWER: Yes, but not until you eradicate the cause of both these killer diseases; and by this we do not mean torture other life forms for the answers for, as long as you carry out such practices, by the laws of the cosmos (karma) other even more perplexing illnesses will be visited upon you. Many of these diseases are what we term 'convenient exit doors'. In other words you undergo unnecessary suffering because you have not been programmed to handle the death syndrome. The natural and dignified way for hominids to transmute (die) would be to arrive at a point at which they knew that the blueprint for that life had been fulfilled and there was nothing further to be gained by staying on in this dimension. They could then bid a temporary farewell to their loved ones and pass peacefully over by a process of will. Do I really need to enumerate the problems that would arise from this in a world of physical and psychological dependencies, selfishness, possessiveness and greed?

Aside from the exit-door aspect, many of your diseases are brought on by yourselves; I am not necessarily referring to the individual, but rather to social conditions, established modes of behaviour, dietary factors, hedonism and, in many parts of your world, starvation and lack of amenities. But it is not my place to criticize and I can only say that, as the realizations of so many" of these facts begin to dawn, you will effect your own cures in more natural ways. In Gaia's garden there is actually a cure for every possible disease and you would be advised to seek therein as, indeed, some of your medical scientists are already doing. But, since many of these diseases are brought on by psychological imbalances, the answers should also be sought within the mind and this will eventually result in an appraisal of your whole social system. In this I cannot and may not interfere, as the full realization of what is taking place must come from within yourselves. I wish you much success in this your great initiation and my love and healing thoughts go out to you all.

QUESTION: Can you give us any more examples, or analogies of the alltime-is-one concept as related to reincarnation. I know Kaini covered this in some detail in *THE LION PEOPLE*, but there are still points that some of us do not understand.

ANSWER: I think I will hand over to Kaini for this one, as it falls more within his province than mine.

KAINI:

TIME AND THE INITIAL COSMIC IMPULSE OR GROUP SOUL:

Time is neither linear nor movable. It radiates in static bands in all directions, above, below, all round, into infinity. The universe of time could be described as one infinite atom, with a timeless-spaceless core that is made up from an infinite number of minute particles. Minute particles in a state of constant movement could be seen to represent interchangeable time-zones and, just as physicists working with quantum mechanics are able to observe quantum leaps in the transition of an atomic or molecular system from one discrete state to another, so this same principle repeats itself at all and every level, including that of human experience. In the same way that physicists have difficulty in knowing when a particle is a particle and when it is a wave, as evidenced in the principle of non-locality, particle/wave packets can represent interchangeable time-zones, which coexist simultaneously like parallel universes and yet retain contact over time and space.

Groups of essences whose fragments have completed their evolutionary cycle eventually accrete until they are once again freed by the natural process of cosmic motion. Once released from the group consciousness or central core each essence embarks on a series of journeys through the outer peripheries of time. These journeys do not necessarily fall into sequences as viewed in terms of linear time; in other words, they may move backwards, forwards, sideways, gathering information as they go. Imagine a reel of film which a camera team have just completed. The director takes a look at the rushes but feels that further inclusions are necessary, so the team go out and film some more footage. The old film is then spliced and the new pieces inserted. And yet the first piece of film was perfectly valid in its own right and anyone viewing it would have an accurate picture of what took place during the first shooting which was, to them, complete. But others viewing the second shooting would see far more and disagree entirely with the earlier viewers as to the film's content. Such is the difference between the view of the cosmos afforded to the mature fragment as against that beheld by a less time-travelled psyche.

Although time is static, the experiences undergone in any time-zone are NOT. They may vary according to which angle and which period in the age and evolution of the essence that that time was viewed and recalled. Let us reduce this to the personal by referring to this aforementioned essence as being composed of many smaller particles, each of which may appear to represent a separate intelligence in its own right. Let us further consider that this essence and its particles are not alone in their time-adventures, since they commence their travels in the company of others of their own kind, a sort of conglomerate of allied particles which together comprise a whole (group soul or cosmic impulse), but when separated assume individual characteristics which, nevertheless, still resonate to the basic group archetype. Each group soul, however, has unique qualities that bind its members together; so strong is this link that it will be acknowledged in any time-zone by the other members or fragments to the extent that its power will supersede consanguine and tribal loyalties to the point of changing time-zones (death).

Group souls and the essence-fragments of which they are composed are not necessarily the same in temperament, taste or expression. The basic nature or archetype of one group may differ considerably from that of another, to the extent that a jarring note enters when contrasting elements are thrown together at close quarters. This being so it is only natural that the fragments of one group may not get along with the fragments of another. In certain timeframes these differences are acknowledged as purely academic, but in more primitive time-zones they become exaggerated to the point of strife, or eventual destruction.

Should one therefore stay within one's own archetype, you may ask? Ideally, yes, but as one slowly negotiates less primitive time-zones one becomes more and more exposed to the differing nature of other fragments; and the lesson to be mastered becomes one of understanding, acknowledging and eventually accepting the ways of others and learning to live with them, by complementing their deficiencies and they yours.

In the time-zone that is the present on your Earth, there are several archetypal groups whose fragments tend to be drawn towards one country or land more than another. Thus national characteristics are born. The differences rub or become abrasive at times and conflicts, ideological, practical, sociological, religious and martial are the end results. In other time-zones, a more mature fragment will ascertain what its group archetype represents and act out that role in a way that is complementary to those of the other groups around it. Thus, the strong man does the lifting, the gifted cook prepares the food, the artist provides the decor or entertains while the food is eaten, the farmer grows that which is necessary to the sustenance of the group, the healer tends the sick, the scientist seeks outwards, the musician soothes; and so forth. When you enter a time-zone in which no labour is worth more or less than another in terms of both intrinsic value and material substance, then and then only will all fragments begin to blend.

To know yourself means to become aware of both your basic group archetype and that which is unique to you. For example, your group soul archetype may indicate a teaching order, while you, as an individual, are best able to express yourself via the collector archetype. So you teach history, or concern yourself with archaeological digs, the published results of which will prove invaluable to society as a whole. Come to know yourself, accept what you are gracefully and with relish; and use what you have to complement the gifts or outputs of those around you. When functioning outside a state of true harmony with your own archetype things may *appear* to go wrong for you and you may feel 'out of gear' as it were. This is due to insecurities and imbalances within yourself and not because some imagined evil force is getting at you. Should you elect to be 'out of gear' for material gains, for example, the very things you seek will elude you and you will never know real happiness.

When speaking of these matters on previous occasions I have likened the whole essence to a complete hologram which, when shattered, produces many fragments each of which carries the original picture, albeit less distinctly. This whole process may also be compared with the continual cycle in which minute particles slowly accrete to form larger conglomerates which in turn coalesce until the mass becomes critical and the ensuing explosion – the 'big bang' in your scientific parlance – once again catapults its contents into the formation of a new cycle in which the process takes place all over again, albeit at a slightly different frequency. Frankly, dear things, your own evolutionary journey works in exactly the same way.

We would now like to introduce you to those from whom we in turn learned and are still learning. We have so far referred to them as the Crystal people for reasons we explained in *THE LION PEOPLE*, but we know they will tell you far more about themselves. You will find their approach, delivery and subject matter quite different from our own, and definitely more technical. However, they assure us that they are well aware of their readership, many of whom are ready to hear what they have to say. So, with love and respect, we hand you over to our cosmic cousins from the Sirius system – the Crystal people.

Chapter 3

INTRODUCING THE CRYSTAL PEOPLE

AN IDENTIFICATION:

The first thing you will want from us is a name or names. We are sorry but we are not identifiable by any of the sonics familiar to your world, so you may call us what you will. We are a twosome and, since we always work in pairs, whatever we say goes for both of us. Our reasons for not communicating sooner were mostly concerned with limitations imposed by the cerebral programming of our channel, which lacked the terms of reference necessary for the conveyance of some of our knowledge. Fortunately, the recent inclusion of new data has widened her scope, thus allowing us a degree of access hitherto denied.

The second point we must make quite clear is that although each of you may have a mental picture of what we might look like we are, in fact, beings of pure energy, or light as you might say, without physical vehicles as you would know them. But, since we once had hominid-type bodies, our memory-banks still retain the imprint of these manifestations which we will project to you for the convenience of recognition. Perhaps we should qualify the term 'light' since light, as you know it, is confined to a given spectrum and the 'light' we may refer to, from time to time, in the context of cosmic identity relates more to a state of *enlightenment* than a projected beam or imagined halo or aura.

The race from which we evolved was not a prolific one such as your own. Our numbers were few and remained constant over the aeons. By your standards of physical beauty we would have seemed almost angelic. Our build was slight, our hair golden and luxuriant, our eyes slanted with colours ranging from blue to golden depending on our caste. We differed from you in that you would not have been able to tell the difference between our males and females. Our species was never afflicted by gender problems as is your own and, consequently, both male and female worked as one. We were always born as twins and not everyone reproduced themselves. We mated to produce our 'eggs' and, once the progeny was of a certain age, we returned to our original twin, with whom we worked for the rest of our physical lives. Unlike the Paschats we were not a tribal people and our caste system was based on skills rather than any one group being better or more highly thought of than another. Neither are we emotionally orientated as are the peoples of Earth and yet we now fully understand how the emotions, if not kept under the control of the will, can wreak havoc in the lives of those dominated by them. This has been one of the lessons that we have had to learn from you.

Our dear Paschat cousins have told you many things concerning the birth and subsequent demise of their own planet, and how we acquired the 'Crystal' appellation. Of course we had our own name for our world, and the nearest word to this in your language would be 'Ashen' or something similarly sounding. However, both the old Paschat and Crystal civilizations are now long gone, although you must understand that everything that has occurred, once it has been etched on the annals of time, is there forever and anyone with a knowledge of time's circuitry may access it immediately at will. Thus we are able to 'become' the Crystal people we were all those millennia ago by your time, so that some of you may recognize us as such and feel at ease with that manifestation. Others, however, will be able to accept us as essences of pure energy, but that will depend on whether they themselves have accessed the faster frequencies in which we now function or, to put it in your wording, are time-travelled essence-fragments or old souls. Old souls are easily recognizable by the breadth of their vision, tolerance and understanding, so those among you who confine your comprehension of the universe to the words contained in one book, the message of one teacher or the precepts of one religion only, without a consideration or study of other points of view, automatically advertise your stage of cosmic development. Not all of the teachers that have influenced your world's beliefs, however, were beings of light, the distinction lying between the imposition of a dogma of mental and spiritual subservience, as opposed to respect for the freedom of the individual and the right of all to seek the Infinite in their own unique way. Sadly, those genuine beings of light who have taught a way to self-godhood often observe their teachings conveniently disregarded after their demise. This is due to the tendency, especially among power-obsessed immature essence-fragments, to ignore the words of a great teacher while purporting to follow in his or her footsteps, in order to keep other people subservient to *them*. So sometimes it is *you,* and not the teacher, who is at fault. The first step along the path to self-godhood involves thinking for yourselves and, as one of your much prized holy books tells you, 'seek and ye shall find'. But do you seek? In most cases, no. You blindly follow, because you have been programmed to do so over many centuries.

But enough of that as we are sure that those of you who have the courage to read these words will be among the few who have stepped out into cosmic consciousness, so our admonitions will not apply to you. But perhaps our words will help you to understand the spiritual plight of those around you, who have not been so fortunate and are still bound by the shackles of outworn dogmas that no longer apply to the children of your planetary host.

'COSMIC GENETIC ENGINEERING':

We are being reminded by our Paschat friends that they have committed us to clearing up certain points regarding your own origins. The first of these concerns the study of what you refer to as genetics and how we introduced one of our genes into Earth hominids. We must confess to being rather amused at your concept of genetic engineering involving surgical procedures taking place in laboratories! How very unsubtle! We do assure you that by the time your planet was ready to receive the quantum leap that involved the Crystal gene, we had long since left our physical world behind us and were functioning in subtle dimensions of a kind many of you may not even have dreamt of.

'MIND':

You speak of 'mind' and yet many of you are unsure as to what 'mind' really is. Mind as we understand it consists of the emissions from that fragment of the basic essence (soul, spirit or transpersonal self) which are decided by the frequency at which the specific fragment is functioning. Thus, the 'mental' energy emitted by a young essence-fragment is mostly concentrated on the 'self', its aims being self-gratification and the acquisition of anything that might aid that cause, as may be evidenced in the self-destructive mechanisms so obvious on your planet at the moment. The more mature the fragment, however (or should we say the more disciplined the mind, although this in itself is hardly an adequate description of what actually takes place), the more the fragment-energies are drawn away from the 'self' and all that that implies in hedonistic terms and the outward channelling process commences. At first, these energies – we think you call them thoughts – proceed from your mind in a haphazard way. You may seek various methods of controlling them, some of which succeed and others not. But until such times as you finally become cognizant of the *modus operandi* there are bound to be periods of intense frustration, just as there are for the child when it takes its first, tentative steps in the pursuance of the upright stance. Once recognized, these 'mind' energies are ejected from the psyche in the form of a blaze of active particle/wave packets which are chaotic until such times as they are actively directed, when they start to accrete. This is what your metaphysicians would term 'making thoughts into realities', while your physicists would have another more practical explanation for it which many of them fail to associate with the mental processes.

It strikes us as strange that natural laws now observed by your scientists are seen to apply to certain areas of exploration only, when in fact they apply equally to *everything* on your planet. We hesitate to use the term 'living' since many of you are scarcely aware that life exists in every *thing* from the minutest particle to the largest body you can conceive of in your present limited concept of the universe! So one of the first lessons you have to learn is that your species is but one of many that are interdependent upon the whole eco-web of life that constitutes the Earth experience. Deny this fact at your peril, as the more enlightened among you are slowly beginning to find out.

MATTER AND ANTIMATTER:

Before we embark on an explanation of the process involved in the transference of the Crystal genetic strain to Earth there is something we must tell you. Your scientists are only too aware that from the birth of your universe, the so-termed 'big bang', there has been more matter than antimatter present. This puzzles them, but then it would since they are thinking at one level only, the particle or physical level. For every particle in the universe there is an antiparticle. This has given rise to many metaphysical concepts and myths concerning twin-souls, the 'higher self' remaining somewhere 'above' and never entering incarnation and so forth. When a particle meets its antiparticle both are *apparently* annihilated, leaving behind only a gamma ray[1] as evidence that they once existed. Now a gamma ray is pure energy and the gamma ray resulting from a coupling of particle and antiparticle continues to exist at the level which the particles have recently taken their leave of. In other words, these two – the particle and antiparticle – have left their mark, or added a tiny quotient of energy to the world they are leaving behind, a personal fingerprint as it were. But, because physicists are convinced that the annihilation has been total, does this mean that they have ceased to exist? Of course not. The act of uniting has automatically changed their frequency to one that is physically imperceptible, with your present technology, that is. They have, in fact, moved beyond the physical worlds and are no longer in need of the experiences offered by those worlds.

Nor have they ascended into some kind of static heaven, for within the cosmos there is no such thing as standing still. All things must constantly move, expand, contract, change, breathe in and out as does the universe at all levels. This great living, breathing entity that encompasses ALL TIME past, present and future into infinite eternity is what you refer to as God, although few of you have any real idea as to what this 'god' actually is. For example, there are no 'hot lines' to it, much as this statement may bruise the ego of many of you. You only ascend to it, or return to it if you prefer it that way, but emulating its creative actions, the true nature of which you will learn once you no longer have need of the experiences afforded by the worlds of physical matter or, as we would say, have passed through the particular frequency of what to you is the visible and therefore real world. However, the embryonic creative factor enters

---

1 [*Author's Note:* A gamma ray (γ ray) is defined as: 'Electromagnetic radiations emitted spontaneously by certain radioactive substances in the process of nuclear transition. They are distinguishable from accompanying a and 1 rays by greater penetrating power and absence of deflection in magnetic and electric fields. They are also formed in particle annihilation. The wavelengths of gamma radiations are characteristic of the substance emitting them and range from 3.9×10^{-10} to 4.7×10^{-13} metre. They form the extreme short-wave end of the known electromagnetic spectrum. *Dictionary of Physics* (Penguin), p. 165.]

each essence-fragment quite early in the evolutionary cycle of the essence, as we will be explaining later. (See Chapter 9.)

Once an essence has met with its antibody and has left the worlds of matter, it is able to direct consciously that stream of active particles that it emits and can exercise this control to create. In other words, that energy that is unique to it that we referred to earlier as `mind' can be manipulated to organize energies functioning at lower frequencies. So you see, you are, in a sense, gods in the making! Which brings us round full circle to our genetic influence upon your planet.

We can anticipate one question that is bound to arise from all this: 'Do we automatically meet our antiparticle on death?' Good gracious, no. Many of what you term `the dead' (and what we would term fragments experiencing temporarily in outer time) are less evolved or cosmically aware than those using bodies (incarnate). When an incarnate being of light, or cosmic identity as our leonine cousins prefer to call them, teaches a class on your planet, the 'space' is filled with many more intelligences than those that occupy the seating accommodation provided in the hall, room or lecture theatre. These may come from many other universal frequencies and not necessarily those associated with the one upon which your own world functions. There are beingnesses, or intelligences, in multiple universes beyond your comprehension, which even your science fiction writers have failed to visualize. Many of you will find this mind-blowing and will retreat to the safety of the beliefs you have been conditioned to accept. But sooner or later you will awaken from your cocoon of ignorance and be enthralled by the life existing beyond its cosy but limiting embrace.

So let us return once again to this supposed genetic engineering. How was it accomplished? In the light of the aforegoing you will see that it is simply a question of pure mind-energy. Anything in the universe can be directed by mind-energy or thought force as you prefer to call it, but with the proviso that the energies of the manipulating force are faster or more powerful than those of the manipulated. A being of light manipulates cosmic energy by organizing chaotic subatomic particles on the one hand and dispersing them on the other. Your ancient Egyptian priests referred to this as the double fire, the fire of solidification and the fire of dispersion, exemplified in the goddesses Isis and Nephthys. Thus all and everything is in a constant state of flux, which is as it should be. Periods of order are automatically followed by periods of chaos, while chaos in turn is eventually self-organizing; and so the cycle starts all over again. You have only to refer to your own history books to observe how this is played out in the affairs of humanity, while any psychologist, or doctor for that matter, will be able to explain to you how it manifests in the individual human condition.

When we knew the time to be right for the injection of a new gene into Earth hominids, using our own spiritual/cosmic energies, or power of mind as you would say, we simply directed material containing the gene in question to Earth via panspermia and the circuitry of time (from ours and your future to your past) and ensured that it was ingested by those humans who were ready to receive it. It was then passed on to their children and gradually infiltrated around your world. Those of you who carry it are destined to be instrumental in helping your planet to take its next step forward and, of course, certain of you will, in due course, receive the next gene from us, which will have the effect of activating a portion of your brains hitherto unused. After this has taken place both we and the Paschats will withdraw, for from then on there will be those among your own kind who will be sufficiently evolved, spiritually, cosmically and somatically, to take charge of the future of your own planet. Then, in a parallel universe not dissimilar to your own, such Earth beings are destined to assume the role that we and the Paschats have played in the evolution of your world. This was known to all the beings of light who have taken bodies on your planet for the purpose of bringing the light of truth to your peoples, but sadly the concept became distorted into the idea that you and you alone are in some way supreme in the universe. We can assure you that in other worlds, both subtle and material, life forms entirely different from your own have assumed similar responsibilities.

ON UFOS:

We feel that this subject has already received mention in earlier pages, but perhaps we can add a little more. Over the centuries, energies emitted from both your planet itself and all living things residing thereon have been chaotic. As any physicist will tell you, chaotic subatomic particle/wave packets, or any other term you may use to describe those pockets of energy that appear to run amok in the subatomic kingdoms (before this book has been out very long there will doubtless be a whole new set of descriptive semantics in popular scientific vogue), are influenced by the observer, so that you never know where or what they are really up to. In days long past, these errant energies would therefore appear in forms recognizable to the observers, or rather what the observer believed he or she would see. Let us take an example. The year is AD 1150 in your time, the time of day is late evening and three men are wending their way wearily home after a hard day's work in the fields. There is an abundance of energy in the atmosphere and, as these men work close to the Earth and are therefore in touch with their own instinctive resources or hindbrain, they become aware of this. Chaotic energy inevitably exercises a profound effect on the autonomic nervous system, producing symptoms of fear and alarm, with the accompanying 'fight or flight' physical output. One man says to the other, 'There is something evil about here, John' his companions agree and they commence to hasten their footsteps in the direction of home and safety. But their own minds are busy at work, creating all sorts of figures they have. been programmed to associate with evil – demons, hobgoblins, fearful monsters, trolls and the like – so much so that they actually bestow these appearances on the errant energies surrounding them, giving them a separate or discrete existence and recognizable form. It is therefore little wonder that those three strong men will, on their return, swear that they all witnessed disturbing phenomena of this nature and warn all and sundry against passing along a certain path after dark because 'strange beings of malign intent do lurk there!'

Put this into the modern context and you have a great deal of your UFO phenomena. We say 'a great deal'; is this meant to imply that all do not fall within this category? It does. You see, there are genuine ET visitors of benign intent, although these are *very few and far between,* and there are also curious beings from parallel worlds similar to your own, who have learned to penetrate the veil that separates one physical universe from another – note our emphasis on the word 'physical'. Beings of pure energy have no need to produce phenomena of this kind, although they are able to in the cause of recognition, or to alleviate fear.

PARALLEL WORLDS AND ANTIPARTICLES:

Just as each of you have an antiparticle waiting to join with you somewhere in the universe, so also does your planet. In fact, its anti-world is very close, so close, in fact, that the two dimensions almost touch at times. Of course you will not see it, because it does not function at the same frequency as your 'real' world, any more than you will see your own antiparticle as a replica of yourself, lurking nearby and waiting nervously to make that final connection that will free you both from the limitations of matter. From a metaphysical standpoint antiparticles are complementary to their corresponding particles and are therefore viewed by some researchers as representing the transpersonal or higher self, with which one can only unite at the end of one's evolutionary journey. The particle/antiparticle merging represents a kind of spiritual individuation or balancing of the yin/yang energies, which serves to free the essence-fragment from the frequencies of dense physical matter, so the two concepts should not be confused.

But to return to your UFO question: we see books in your libraries that describe terrible experiments supposedly carried out on people who claim to have been abducted by aliens. Is there any truth in these reports? The answer must be yes and no. Our earlier explanation covers some of them in that there are psychokinetic energies and natural phenomena at work in much the same way that a believer in a certain faith can produce stigmata simply by thinking hard about it, or electrical inconsistencies in the atmosphere can produce weird effects. But you can also blame some of these phenomena on your own actions. Just as you test your chemicals and weapons of destruction on other species, so also do certain aliens, who view some of the people they have observed in much the same way that you see your laboratory animals. But then humanity is nothing if not guilty of speciesism. 'As ye sow so shall ye reap!' Our channel will never forgive us for our constant allusions to the reference book of a certain religion, but we choose to use these as they are better known than some more apt quotes from more obscure books of wisdom.

We can anticipate many of you saying, 'Goodness, we are being bombarded on all sides by a combination of the bizarre creations of our own errant thoughts and suspect cosmic interlopers; what chance do we stand of survival against such odds?' More than you might imagine, for when your own world is cleaned up, as indeed it will be in the not-too-distant future, the new range of frequencies attained will inhibit the manifestation of less desirable intruders from other parts of the cosmos.

QUESTION: What happens when Earth eventually meets with its antiparticle or anti-Earth?

ANSWER: Disintegration. When union is effected, the governing essences will become as one soul and leave the material universe in the same way as we have described for the individual. By this time, all life as you know it will have departed, and only the bare shell of your planet will remain. As the universe breathes in, so will all matter within a given region of frequency be drawn ultimately into what your scientists refer to as 'the big crunch'; but a word of advice: while your particular universe is experiencing a big crunch another is experiencing a big bang. We would express this in a sine wave thus:

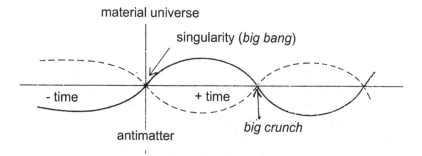

Sine waves crossing

Then there are countless dimensions, each with its own sine wave and rhythmic respirations which vary in length, amplitude and phase. Believe us, there are universes in existence the knowledge of which would frighten you in your present stage of development, just as a nuclear explosion, or even your Christmas town fairy lights, would have proved all too much for the people of AD 1200!

QUESTION: But what about our Moon. Is that not a dead sphere and yet it is still there?

ANSWER: Do not judge what is dead or alive by what you can see. Rest assured there are life-forms on your Moon, although you would not recognize them as such. But then there are many things that are visible to the denizens of faster frequencies than your own that you may not observe from where you are placed on the cosmic scale; well, for the time being, anyway.

QUESTION: Is there any way we can protect ourselves against these unfriendly aliens, wherever they come from, or even if they are the result of our own unbridled thoughts? Can we call on you for protection, for example?

ANSWER: You can if you so wish, but in the final analysis your best protection lies in your own hands. The way you live, the life you lead, your eating, drinking and social habits, all these go to erect a barrier against alien intrusion, or the reverse since like inevitably attracts like. And, remember, alien intrusion does not simply manifest as bug-eyed monsters or little green men who zap people with death rays from strange shaped space-ships. In fact, it is much more likely to enter in the form of a killer disease that attacks people worldwide; think about it and you will recognize it!

QUESTION: Do you come in UFOs these days?

ANSWER: No, we do not, since there is no need. As beings off pure energy we communicate direct, mind to mind.

QUESTION: Do you and the Paschats have members of your species incarnate among us and, if so, are you able to protect them?

ANSWER: Yes, we do. And we are able to protect them against *any alien or chaotic energy that might interfere with the work they have incarnated to do,* but that is all. In other words, we cannot single them out for special treatment by protecting them against the everyday contingencies of life on Earth, such as the normal emotional responses that form part and parcel of the Earth hominid experience. These they must suffer and observe and in so doing they add to the knowledge of their own cosmic impulse or group soul. In fact there is one of them typing this as we dictate it. Originally of the feline/Paschat impulse, she has also worked with us closely in our 'nuts and bolts' space pioneering days, which we left behind aeons ago. When her time comes to vacate her present Earth body, her antiparticle awaits her demise and together we and our Paschat friends will leave for other dimensions.

51

QUESTION: Could you tell us more about the state following death. For example, what happens to those souls who are not yet completely ready to leave the world of matter, but who have finished a particular cycle of incarnations. Or do you not go along with that teaching?

ANSWER: We have no argument with that teaching. In fact, were you to read the teachings given by those enlightened ones who have visited your Earth from time to time you would find this well expressed. People read what they want to read and either ignore that which does not accord with their own pet theories, or miss the point because they are not ready to absorb such knowledge. I will ask my channel if she can produce some references to such teachings. She says she can. Will she then reproduce these here and now? She says yes.

MURRY: I am reproducing the following extract from a book entitled *Immortal Sisters: Secrets of Taoist Women* at the request of the Crystal people:

'A classic exposition of the humanitarian aspect of Taoism is to be found in the story of the distinguished Immortal Sister Zhao of the Song Dynasty (960-1278 C.E.). The question of charitable works was raised by her brother after he had overheard her receiving esoteric instructions on rainmaking. He asked her why spiritual immortals, who had transcended the mundane world, would bother to do such things as make rain. Immortal Sister Zhao replied, "those who have now attained spiritual immortality but cannot as yet live in heaven number in thousands. They are all in various places on earth accumulating virtue, carrying out practical undertakings so that they may eventually make the ascent.

'Some of them take care of rivers and lakes, some of them manage the hidden government, some are in charge of mountains. They work to benefit ten thousand generations, to rid the earth of what is harmful, to heal the sick and eliminate problems, acting mercifully towards the troubled and uplifting the fallen, rescuing the weak and helpless.

'Their hidden works are carried out in secret, their virtuous deeds are practised covertly. Such is their range that they cannot be encompassed in one generation. But the spiritual immortals do not take pride in themselves, and are wary of becoming known to the public; therefore worldly people do not get to hear about them.'[1] This is but one example, there are several others, notably in the G.R.S. Mead translation of the *Hermes Trismegistus*. I will now hand back to the Crystal people.'

QUESTION: Are you telling us that discarnate hominid souls work with the spirits of the elements, trees, rivers and so forth? We ask this as we have always been taught that the elemental kingdoms and devas were of a different evolutionary strain.

ANSWER: Your teaching is correct, for so they are. But this does not mean that at a higher level of consciousness several different kinds of intelligences cannot work together. In fact, the essence of evolution is the slow integration of all species into a complete and whole understanding. Speciesism, like racism, is a young-soul trait.

HEAVEN:

The reference to 'heaven' in those lines might well arouse the curiosity of some of our readers. In the context of our message, of course, it refers to the complete freeing of the essence from the bonds of matter resulting from its meeting with the antiparticle. If any of you really thought that the processes of nature occur randomly and without a directional impulse, then we must enlighten you otherwise. There is 'mind' of some kind behind every purpose, which might at face value appear to contradict our 'chaotic energy' theory. In fact, it does not, because even chaotic energy falls under the observation of and therefore the direction of something or other, just as it is easily ensouled by your own chaotic thought patterns as they career wildly around the aura of your planet. You may be totally unaware of what you are actually contributing to the whole, but contribute to it you do, in one way or other.

QUESTION: The Paschats tell us that your race originally carried a fire/air emphasis, whereas the Paschats themselves are fire/earth. Could you tell us something about the elemental emphases on our own planet, Earth?

---

1 *Immortal* Sisters. Translated and edited by Thomas Cleary, p.5

ANSWER: Look around your planet and what do you see? A preponderance of water. Look at your own bodies, they carry a high fluid content. Earth hominids are decidedly emotionally orientated, although those emotions may not be directed towards the more popular concepts of emotional outlets such as romance, hysteria and so forth. The seemingly hard-headed executive who has little time for the sentimental is as emotionally involved in his business as the mother is with her baby or the lover with his lass! Emotional excesses are exhibited in apparently unemotional pursuits such as the worship of machinery – cars, motor bikes, computers. Many a rich man prizes his racing car above his lover, wife or children. Likewise, both men and women who eschew the world around them in favour of a closed religious life are pouring their emotions into the faith to which they subscribe. Your women are frequently emotionally dominated by their progeny to the point of irrationality. Your other element is, of course, earth, which speaks for itself in your obsession with material possessions. It should be understood, however, that individuals within the hominid collective naturally carry varying distinctive quotients of elemental qualities in each life, which may be easily viewed in the birth chart.

You refer to your planet in the feminine as Gaia, taking the name from your ancient Greek mythology. Unfortunately, this name does not really resonate to the sonic of the entity that is your Earth. One of your prehistoric civilizations effected a nearer match when they called her Danuih. However, you are finally on the right track in acknowledging her existence as a self-regulating entity in her own right, who could eject your species tomorrow if she so wished. But like her hominid progeny she is also water-orientated, which is why she has forgiven you so much. So in a way you can thank the overemotionalism to which your species is subject for the fact that *you* are still here, although had you and your planet been more airy or fiery you would not have accepted the afflicting virus in the first place.

QUESTION: In *THE LION PEOPLE* Kaini said, 'We are silent watchers and thus we protect, but when it becomes necessary for us to strike in defence it is with the strength of the lion and the skill and speed of the cheetah.' You mentioned earlier that you protect your own; what methods would you use and could you tell us more about how the Paschats would protect their own?

ANSWER: Fear is such a prevalent emotion on your planet that you instinctively sense predators at every corner. Many of the ups and downs you experience have nothing whatsoever to do with being 'attacked' by ETs or what you would term 'occult' forces as they are, more often than not, rebounds from your own thoughts and actions. We suggested that we would protect our own kind if their work, and therefore ours, is ever threatened. This we would not achieve by the use of phenomena guaranteed to attract public attention. Quite the reverse, in fact. We would simply insure their removal to less tensive pastures by natural processes such as a change of work pattern or financial circumstances that call for certain relocations. Since there are comparatively few Crystal people incarnate in Earth bodies at present and these have all been strategically placed anyway, we have few problems, as our people, being of a basic hominid impulse, do not experience all that much difficulty in adjusting to Earth existence, as long as the environment is of a certain kind. The Paschats have even fewer operatives in hominid bodies but they, poor things, do not have an easy time. Paschats are by nature outgoing and warm hearted. Unlike our race they also formed strong family ties, as do your primitive lions with their prides, and to be rejected as 'odd' causes them much pain. Your people are very quick to pick up an alien influence in an Earth body and incarnate Paschat entities are often either liked or hated on sight, usually depending on whether the people they encounter are cat lovers. A discarnate Paschat entity protecting its own can produce some very strange and rather frightening effects, as our channel has found to her amusement! But we would not recommend any of you to put it to the test.

QUESTION: Could you protect us physically or psychically if we called on you for help?

ANSWER: We are always pleased to help anyone who asks but, as we have already stated, the way in which we would dispense that assistance might not be quite what Earth hominids would prefer, since most of the prayers and rites we hear are usually for a problem to be miraculously resolved with as little effort as possible on the part of the supplicant. Our approach to your requests would be by way of trying to help you to help yourselves, which involves, among other things, not courting danger in the first place. But please feel free to approach us if you so wish.

Chapter 4

THE CRYSTAL PEOPLE

SCIENCE AND THE OCCULT.

We, whom you call the Crystal people, continue our discourse with some comments on what, you refer to as 'magic' and the 'occult'. For us there are no such things and you would be wiser to view these metaphysical studies for what they really are, a body of knowledge concerned with natural, cosmic laws which, due to an overemphasis on the worlds of physical matter, has become severed from the scientific mainstream. So-termed 'occult mysteries' are therefore nothing more or less than ancient scientific facts that became encoded into terms of reference easily understood by the unlettered, many of which, over the centuries, degenerated into superstition, their true meaning having been long since forgotten. It falls to us to decode some of these for you and relate them to their true perspective.

'Magic' and 'occult' energy, to use your own terms, work at three main levels.
1. The manipulation of particle aggregates (matter) via the agency of mind.
2. The conscious negotiation of particle/wave packets in non-locality (subtle energies on the inner planes in your magical parlance).
3. Imitating certain basic universal principles or patterns, which can have the effect of setting corresponding events into motion at the physical level, a process referred to as 'sympathetic' magic.

Regarding (1), were your planet on its correct evolutionary course this faculty would be in fairly general use by now and not the exclusive domain of the metaphysician and 'performer'. In fact, the extent to which this is used among you with any degree of efficiency is miniscule, when judged against your true potential and compared with the psychokinetic powers exhibited by races known to us in other parts of the universe. In plain words, your knowledge of this practice is in its infancy. It could be argued that there are a few individuals who do possess extraordinary powers but these only *appear* impressive because you have no idea of your ultimate capabilities in this field, or the range these will ultimately cover. To give you an example from our own physical past, when the second Sun in our solar system collapsed into a white dwarf we were able to contain and channel the enormous energies emitted during the course of its transformation *by mind control pure and simple.* No technology of any kind was employed in this process. Such mental powers are also *your* natural heritage and in future years you will learn how to acknowledge their existence and utilize them wisely.

As for (2), we regret to inform you that the number of adepts capable of this function could be counted on one hand *over the whole history of your planet.* So don't be too taken in by the 'amazing feats' that were supposedly carried out by prehistoric civilizations.' Agreed, there were those around in early times who were capable of influencing matter, but the manipulation of nonlocal components requires a mastery of the circuits of time and we would be less than honest if we were to lead you to believe otherwise.

On the other hand (3) has been effectively practised by primitive (and not so primitive since many of you are still doing it today) Earth hominids since the dawn of time and, although it can and does produce some results, these are minimal compared with (1) and (2).

Another capacity that is often confused with matters `occult' is shown in the many manifestations of the use of the intuitive faculty or right brain promptings which you classify under the headings of extra sensory perception. Whether you are reading cards, runes, practising psychometry, or simply endeavouring to communicate with some entity from another waveband, the facility you are employing is the same. Only the frequency at which it is used differs and, of course, we must also point out that much of what passes as clairvoyance and allied receptive phenomena is nothing more or less than wishful thinking. Our leonine cousins have previously commented on this in some detail, but we are sure that if you have further questions they will be only too pleased to elucidate. They have made a special study of the psychology of Earth hominids and are therefore well equipped to handle your queries.

ALTERED STATES OF CONSCIOUSNESS:

There is a mistaken impression among many of you that anything viewed or experienced during an ASC must be valid. This is not necessarily the case, especially with ASCs that have been induced by some unnatural means. The mind can only transmit to the brain that which it is capable of absorbing according to the cosmic age of the essence-fragment and, once that ring-passnot has been attained, all that is left for it is to move sideways, as it were. Experiencing an altered state of consciousness is no guarantee of (a) spirituality, (b) psychic or magical prowess, (c) cosmic maturity. Another piece of information that might interest you is that the lot of the mature essencefragment incarnate on your planet is not now nor ever has been an easy one. Old souls, as you prefer to call them, are seldom comfortable in your material world for several reasons. Firstly, they carry memories of a kinder, more caring way of living which, when compared with your own, causes them much mental anguish. Secondly, your values have little meaning to them so they are seldom achievers in the material sense. If you look back at the lives of those you acknowledge as Masters you will find few who were born into wealth and those that were have hastened to eschew it and opt for a simple living regime. The excessive accumulation of material goods and possessions is not the hallmark of cosmic maturity and we are sorry if this offends some of you. But neither is the other extreme, whereby people neglect the cleanliness of their persons and living quarters, ignore or abuse the requirements of the components of their bodies and soil the corpus of your planet whom you call Gaia with their personal and industrial filth and refuse. If we seem to criticize your ways too much it is for your own benefit in the long run, as your time in your present mode is fast running out.

RITUAL:

Ritual would appear to be a prerequisite for many of you seeking the transcendental. Ritual, of course, is not the exclusive property of the magical fraternity, or the religious fraternity come to that. You each perform rituals in your everyday life, albeit unconsciously at times, so it would be fair to say that a limited amount of ritual is a healthy aid to mental and physical discipline. Where ritual goes 'over the top', however, is when it becomes a prop or a dependency. For example, many people are unable to conceive of a higher power, or obtain an altered state of consciousness, without the aid of ritual, which is all wrong. Ritual is one of the signposts we all pass along the infinite road of evolution. But so, also, is the solitary experience, the private ASC, the personal battle with chaos; and so forth. When overshadowing our channel while she was writing *The Psychology of Ritual* (she was not aware at that time who we were, other than that we were 'of the light') we pointed. out to her that the rite's power to affect body chemistry is in the nature of a somatic mismanagement; so that the participation in the ecstatic venture via the avenues of ritual can be as much madness as enlightenment and therefore highly misleading, the dividing line between frenzy and ecstasy being so tenuous as to be indefinable. If you are unable to reach out to whatever may be your concept of the divinity without being entertained by the paraphernalia of ornate vestments, emotionally stimulating music, powerful scents, chants, drumbeats, or whatever, then fair enough. But eventually the time will come, at some stage in your spiritual journey, when you will become aware that the divinity you have been seeking is not part and parcel of some extramundane transcendental experience, but is there around you all the time, in the smiling face of a flower, the soft fur of an animal, the sheltering arm of a mighty tree. And in so knowing and understanding you will be centered by the realization that the Creator is ALL and EVERYTHING and not some distant, inaccessible state that can only be approached through the trappings of material wealth! Likewise the aspiring magician will come to understand that the most powerful magic of all is created within his or her own mind. But ritual is, as we have said, a gateway through which most have passed at some time or other; so, if you must perform your rites, do ensure that you are sufficiently familiar with what you are doing to be able to distinguish between the qualities and frequencies of the energies you invoke or evoke and, what is more important, that you have the strength of mind to cope with whatever is forthcoming. For, remember, like inevitably attracts like!

RADIOACTIVITY AND DNA:

We have frequently heard you ask about the effects of radioactivity on DNA, especially in relation to the forthcoming pole shift and quantum leap. Radioactivity certainly affects DNA and, therefore, any increase is potentially dangerous. However, it does play an important role in evolutionary quantum leaps in that a high increase in radioactivity precipitates genetic mutation in DNA and, as that mutation takes place, it will inhibit the quality or frequency of the ensouling energy or consciousness, thus raising the evolutionary level of the matter in question. The more tolerant the DNA is to radioactivity, the more advanced the incoming evolutionary stream, which renders radioactivity a deciding factor in quantum jumps.

Of course, this also affects animal and plant life on a planet: the more mature the essence-fragment the higher the tolerance. In other words, different lifeforms are capable of higher tolerance in their more advanced manifestations in other star systems. For example, a cat or dog can tolerate the present rate of radioactivity on your planet, their wave-aspects (spirits/psyches) being in a fairly low stage of development when compared with the frequencies of their fragments elsewhere in the universe. But on another physical planet they could tolerate a much higher rate if their essence-fragments were manifesting in a more cosmically mature mode. Much also depends on the predominating element in any evolutionary stream, as has already been explained to you, while another factor to be taken into consideration when one is dealing with the mind-matter relationship is that according to cosmic law physical systems function within set frequencies, depending on the overall nature of the particular universe. For example, in your universe, what you recognize as consciousness, when attached to mass, can only function within the limitations of that mass. At absolute zero, hypothetically speaking, mass would become unstable and any consciousness attached to it would be automatically ejected; the same also applies at the other end of the scale.

May we ask our channel to quote you a short extract from Professor Hoyle's book, *The Intelligent Universe,* which may help to qualify what we are trying to say:
'Quantum mechanics is based on the propagation of radiation only from past to future, and as we have seen leads only to statistical averages. Quantum mechanics is no exception to general experience in physics, which shows that the

propagation of radiation in the past-to-future time-sense leads inevitably to degeneration, to senescence, to the loss of information. It is like leaving a torch switched on. The beam, initially bright, gradually fades away, and eventually it vanishes. But in biology this situation is reversed, because as living organisms develop they increase in complexity, gaining information rather than losing it. It is as if a torch could spontaneously collect light, focus it into a bulb, convert it into electricity and store it.

'How can living organisms manage this. I think we must abandon our preconceptions to appreciate what is happening. If the familiar past-to-future time-sense were to lie at the root of biology, living matter would like other physical systems be carried down to disintegration and collapse. Because this does not happen one must conclude, it seems to me, that biological systems are able in some way to utilize the opposite time-sense in which radiation propagates from future to past. Bizarre as this may appear, they must somehow be working *backwards* in time.'[1]

Thank you, Murry. Perhaps the aforegoing will help our readers to grasp the fact that time's arrow is multidirectional, and all consciousness throughout all universes utilizes it as required, either consciously or unconsciously, according to its stage of cosmic maturity. Conscious manipulation, however, indicates a knowledge of time's circuitry or in your metaphysical parlance - an old soul. We will be discussing biological systems with you in the next chapter, but now it is time for your questions, so please proceed.

QUESTION: The recent identification of quasi-crystals has caused quite a stir in scientific circles as they do not appear to conform to the symmetry of normal crystals. Could you tell us more about them and why they have only recently been discovered?

ANSWER: We prefer the word 'rediscovered' as they were known to the scientist-priests of prehistoric civilizations. If you read the information available on them you will see that they are non-periodic and therefore do not tile in the same way as conventional crystals. Being five-sided, there are inevitably gaps, although one of your scientists has offered an ingenious tiling system using two shapes,

---

1 Hoyle, Fred. *The Intelligent Universe*, pp.212-213.

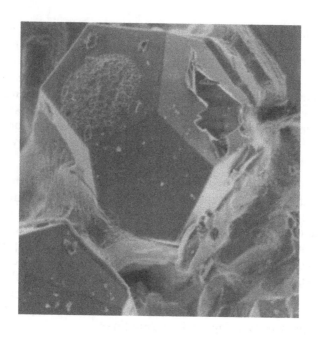

a fat rhombus and a thin rhombus. We draw your attention to two factors here: firstly, the order in these crystals is long range and, secondly, the spaces caused by the lack of fit are highly significant. It is not part of our teaching to point your scientists in any particular direction, but one tiny hint we could offer is that they consider the 'spaces' in terms of storage units. Unfortunately our channel does not have the knowledge of advanced mathematics necessary to effect the equation for this but, rest assured, we do have one of our own people positioned in the scientific establishment who will bring it through at exactly the right time. We would also beg you to consider these natural structures as having a macrocosmic correspondence which should provide you with some clues regarding the much sort after 'dark matter' and those enigmatic 'holes' in space. All in all quasi-crystals hold the key to quite a few cosmological mysteries, as well as possessing properties and an energy potential as yet unrecognized and therefore untapped! And while on the subject of economic energy storage here is our tip for the future: superconductivity! Enough said.

QUESTION: If time becomes infinite when the speed of light is achieved, what happens when all motion is stopped; should not infinity again be achieved? If so, then ultimate speed and ultimate inactivity are the self-same (the usual definition of space and time?).

ANSWER: Dare we suggest that the questioner is not too sure of the nature of his question? Theoretical physicists may well produce equations for timelessness but to date they have little if any evidence of what does happen beyond the speed of light. What they do know, however, is that as an object approaches the speed of light it increases in mass and therefore in energy. But as that mass is finite by nature, by the laws of physics it will never actually reach the speed of light. Only waves that carry no mass (matter) are therefore seen as being able to move at the speed of light. This premise is both correct and incorrect. It is correct because mankind will not be able to pass the speed of light in his present stage of technological (and somatic) development, but incorrect in that in the future each and every one of you will have subtle bodies of insufficient mass to enable you to pass that point in the natural process of your evolutionary development, by which time your technology will have solved the problem, anyway. There is also a third factor involved, which is the negotiation of time's circuitry, but again we must say that you do not at present possess either the mental know-how or technology to achieve this, neither will you until you come to understand that all universes, like all time, exist simultaneously and within each other. However, your questioner is correct in his surmise that the laws of motion change drastically at both ends of the space-time spectrum.

QUESTION: In the collision chamber the tracks of high energy particles are mapped by a high speed camera. These slow particles have been accelerated and the charged particles are shown as spirals that appear to have a beginning and an end. Where do they go at the end of their journey? I suggest that they disappear again by slowing down, indicating that there is a universe (or universes), that functions at a lower vibrational frequency than our own; in which case another universe or universes functioning at a higher speed could be 'seen' in a decelerator?

ANSWER: Goodness, we are getting technical here, are we not. We rather feel you have answered this question for yourself. Minute particles appear to be in a constant state of *flux because they are minute,* observable speeds being relevant to the observer. Were you to view the universe from the position we are in, you would be able to see whole universes (and there are an infinite number of these, in addition to the manifestation of matter at a speed complementary to your own that you are able to view in your night sky and attribute to the singularity you refer to as the big bang) moving at speeds not dissimilar to those encountered in your particle accelerators. Cosmic speeds are relevant to the viewing of the beholder. As you watch your night sky you do not see the physical universe rushing about all over the skies; and yet cosmologists will tell you that they are able to ascertain from their calculations that the whole universe is moving at immense speeds! And you should also remember that you are no different from the particles or galaxies.

We have heard it suggested that mature essence-fragments, like galaxies, travel in spirals, while their younger aspects proceed in straight lines. In a sense this is true but again such correspondences are only comparative because, at a certain level, time *appears* to be moving in a straight line and it is only when you, we, or anything else in the universe start to move into the faster range of frequencies that its multidirectionality becomes obvious. By energizing your own mental frequencies you may *appear* to gain access to what you refer to as 'higher vibrations', but equally the energies you emit can act upon those that are normally imperceptible to your present waveband and slow them down sufficiently for them to become momentarily perceptible! In other words, it can work from both ends.

QUESTION: I have just read about some very recent discoveries by Margaret Geller and John Huchra which suggest that the galaxies are arranged in thin sheets wrapped around enormous voids, some of which are as big as the one in Bootes. Geller describes the pattern as resembling soap bubbles, or perhaps a sponge. Both astro-physicists are now confronted with the question as to what this strange cosmic architecture implies. Some astronomers have suggested that these so-termed 'voids' are not empty at all, but filled with a mysterious invisible substance called cold dark matter, which has already been proposed as a kind of gravitational 'glue' to hold galaxies and clusters of galaxies together. Some experts think that this dark matter may account for more than 90 per cent of the substance of the universe, but the main problem is that this is all theory and cold dark matter has yet to be discovered. We are told that 12,000 galaxies have been charted to date and 300 million light years at the least are involved. Comments, please?

ANSWER: Your scientists have certainly come up with a variety of 'patterns' for the universe over the past few years, each varying in the light of more refined instrumentation and technology. We cannot tell you much about this particular phenomenon as our channel does not possess the necessary terms of reference and, come to that, neither do your scientists, who are not agreed about it among themselves. But suffice it to say that dark matter has transmutatory properties – antimatter being one – while also containing more than one characteristic that is alien to present scientific thinking. Metaphysically speaking, it is concerned with a species of intelligent entities whom we will loosely refer to as archons, about which we will tell you more later. (See Chapter 9.)

The physical universe as observed and plotted by your scientists is only one minute aspect of the cosmos and, as has already been explained to you, you are able to observe it because you resonate at the same frequency. Before scientists can unravel the mystery of dark matter they will have to adjust their ideas to the fact that there are universes that are not observable *physically,* although theoretical physicists and mathematicians will produce equations appropriate to their existence. You will not be able to negotiate or investigate these worlds until you come to understand the true nature of time, which will facilitate your ability to move from one universe to another *by adjusting to the frequency in question.* This is technologically possible up to a certain point, beyond which you will be faced with the enigma of pure metaphysics. But by that time the people of Earth will be sufficiently right-brain orientated to handle the problem.

Rest assured, however, that no matter how many millions of galaxies are discovered there are still more, *ad infinitum,* and yes, they do form a certain symmetry which may appear chaotic from the microcosmic angle but is ultimately macrocosmically orderly. Since the macrocosm is always reflected in the microcosm, the shape and formations of galaxies may be evidenced in some mundane pattern exhibited in your everyday lives, as Dr.Geller has so wisely observed in her soap-bubble analogy. We are sorry to insist, however, that there is no 'edge' of the universe and 'big bangs' and 'big crunches' are going on all the time, that relating to the birth and eventual demise of your particular universe being but one of many in the ever continuing creative process of dissolution/dispersion and coalescence/solidification. And, remember, *nothing within this entire process ever ceases to exist, it is simply transformed.* We appreciate this is difficult for the finite mind to grasp, but rest assured that future generations of Earthlings will accept it as easily as you accept the technology of your present world, which would have been deemed 'impossible' a century or so ago in your time.

QUESTION: Why does the creator allow chaos to exist?

ANSWER: It neither allows nor disallows anything. It purely emits energy that is at the same time both orderly and chaotic. You see, chaotic energies act as solvents and, although they may appear at close quarters to be purely destructive, especially if they are out of balance with the time-zone in which they are manifesting, they are essential to the continual growth of the universe in that they contribute to the perpetual motion that keeps the whole of creation in equipoise. They ensure that nothing stagnates, that the order/chaos sequence is always observed in balance so that there is a chance for everything to undergo myriad infinite experiences. There are scientific laws that are concerned with the manifestation of chaos at the personal level. We think it better if our dear Mikili explains these to you, perhaps in the next chapter if our channel will so allow.

COLLECTIVE IDENTITIES:

Let us now abandon the questions for a while and consider some of the other problems that beset both metaphysician and layman alike, especially in the light of the changing climate of opinion concerning the role of mankind in the evolution of Gaia and vice versa.

When a person makes a machine, the components of that machine are made up of a series of singular identities which, when blended together, form a collective unit which assumes a group identity. In making this machine and putting it into use the man or woman becomes a creator in his or her own right and that machine affords experience to both the creator and the collective identity of the individual particles/molecules encapsulated therein. A link is also formed between the created and the creator which continues regardless of time and space, as may be evidenced in your Einstein-Podolski-Rosen paradox.

Likewise the energies or essences that create or bring together the cohesive molecular intelligences which constitute a genotype have exactly the same relationship with their creation. In this way cosmic bonds are forged and the principle involved permeates all levels from the humblest to the most sublime. Those beings who had a hand in the creation of Gaia, and your solar system for that matter, are bound to their creation by this rule, which is why your mystics have been bombarded over the centuries with teachings that appear to flow contrary to what you broadly describe as 'human nature'. We regret to tell you that it is not the teachers of wisdom who are wrong, but 'human nature', which is not as 'natural' as you would believe. In fact it is highly unnatural because it is tainted by a virus, as our leonine friends have already explained. The animal and plant kingdoms are less tainted than hominids, however, although even within their ranks there are deviants, as the original blueprint did not allow for the predatory habits of many species. It amuses us when we hear those of you who own cats or dogs complaining when your pet brings in a bird, mouse or rabbit, while you tuck into your side of beef! Perhaps if you had to go out and hunt for it yourself you might change your ideas and your eating habits!

Just as human collectives are composed of individuals, each in his or her own stage of cosmic development, all other life forms on your planet are likewise composed of numerous intelligences, each with its own individuality. The bodies of your pets may house mature or youthful fragments, which is why some animals display gentler and more caring tendencies than others. One of the signs of the immature psyche is a love of noise. Just as the young child often amuses itself by creating as much din as possible, so do young essencefragments betray their soul-age by seeking noise as a stimulant, and displaying a marked tendency to avoid silence at all cost. For the mature essence-fragment, silence in abundance is essential and it is exactly the same with animals.

THE ROLE OF THE GHOST IN THE MACHINE:

Taken in the above context the human body is also a machine which consists of a collection of individual molecules seemingly ordered by a computer you call a brain. But who is responsible for that creation once it is in existence, and who programmes the computer: the parents, the genes, or the environment? The essence-fragment or psyche should effect these responsibilities via the mind. In fact, to the molecules, particles and elements within your bodies, the major organs through which they function and the various other minute life-forms that occupy your person YOU are GOD, and as such are fully responsible for their efficient and cohesive working. Therefore, when you abuse your body in any way, those entities will view you either as a tyrannical ruler, or as divinity whom they have in some way offended. And, if you push them too hard, then they will withdraw *their* essence-fragments, which will result in your early demise.

What we are trying to point out to you is that everything in the whole universe is inextricably linked, all manifestations of consciousness being obligated in some way towards each other. There are no `free rides' and shirked responsibilities must inevitably be faced up to since the links, once forged, cannot be dropped. Sooner or later, somewhere in the infinity of time and space, they will demand redress. This is what you call 'karma'.

THE CHAKRA CONCEPT:

We hear you speak of chakras, asserting that you have seven of these which link your soma with its etheric counterpart. We would question the number, but that is another subject. What we wish to explain to you at this moment in time is that just as you view these as channels of communication between your bodies and other, more subtle dimensions, so also does your planet have similar connections with your solar system, the solar system with the galaxy, the galaxy with other parts of the universe and so forth *ad infinitum.* Gaia links with her parent Sun through a centre that is located very near to your own country, while your star in turn links with its parent, the giant blue-white star you call Sirius. Please note that all 'parent' stars are by polarity female. Your Sun is not the masculine force you imagine, although it accommodates a masculine aspect to its personality. The only time you are likely to encounter a masculine sun is in a system containing more than one star, such as the binary 'seed' system from which we originally hailed. *Perhaps we* could dispense with this masculine/feminine terminology and refer to these energies in the Chinese idiom of yang/yin, which is surely much less inflammatory, bearing in mind the present climate of opinion among both sexes on your planet.

This seems as good a point as any to hand back to our leonine cousins, who will tackle some of the more personal and less technical questions you have for us all.

Chapter 5

MIKILI

PASCHAT EVOLUTION AND GAIA'S ANIMAL KINGDOMS:

Here, my dear ones, is a question we frequently hear you asking, especially after you have been watching films about wildlife: are Paschats anything like the lions or cats on your planet and did we evolve from similar creatures? As we have explained in previous communications, the particular species that is destined to become dominant on any planet that houses life as you know it is decided by the nature of the creative essence responsible for the birth and growth of that planet. For example, in our star system, *as it used to be prior to the collapse of the second Sun,* dual influences prevailed, these being hominid and leonid (or feline as you might prefer to call it), both of which had their origins in other galaxies. The hominid influence developed to dominance on the Crystal planet and the feline on our old home planet. However, on both the planets concerned there were highly evolved beings in existence prior to the arrival of the Crystal people and ourselves. On the Crystal planet there was an advanced mineral strain, while on our planet the tree and plant people had reached a high stage of spiritual development when we arrived there. Thus the ground was prepared by older essence-fragments for the younger ones that were to come.

This should also have occurred on your planet, the ground being prepared by the lizard strain from the Capella region of Auriga, a gentle and highly evolved race. However, after they had completed their work of conveying the necessary DNA to Earth, the first effects of the aforementioned cosmic virus started to make themselves felt and, as a result, certain genetic mutations took place among the early saurians that prevented their somas evolving to a stage that would

70

allow entry to more mature essence-fragments. As a consequence the species degenerated into the dinosaurs which your planet was forced eventually to evict from her surface; with the help of certain bodies external to her normal environment, I might add!

I can hear the more sceptical among you saying, 'But surely the dinosaurs existed a long time before mankind was about, so how can you reconcile this with your former comments concerning the hominid infection by the virus?'

The dinosaurs reigned for more than 100 million years, dominating life on land during the Mesozoic era, about 250 to 66 million years ago. Your word 'dinosaur' is derived from a Greek word meaning 'monstrous lizard'. The Mesozoic period gave way to the Cenozoic, a time when mammals were due to make their appearance on your planet but, unfortunately for the early mammals, because they were not welcomed by their destined spiritual inheritance, evolutionary adjustments had to be effected. This constituted the second impediment to Gaia's growth. The Crystal people were due to take over from the Lizard people in helping with the development of the species that was ultimately to become dominant on your planet but, because the evolved Lizard essence-fragments had been unable to prepare the ground properly for the arrival of the mammals and therefore the advent of the hominid species, the Crystal entities from Sirius were unable to carry out their specific tasks, which were to have consisted of refining and reshaping the hominid bodies to a standard at which they would be eventually ready to receive more mature essence-fragments. You see, your Earth was not originally designed to be a hominid cosmic nursery. There are plenty of that kind of planet dotted around your own and other galaxies. If Gaia was on her correct evolutionary course and, therefore, those incarnate upon her were of the stage of evolution written into the original blueprint for your present time and age, you would all be gifted with second sight, there would be no aggression either among people or animals, your living and eating habits would be entirely different, and Gaia would not have undergone the terrible suffering that your kind have inflicted upon her over the centuries.

So let us get back to the question of your wild animals such as lions, tigers, jaguars, pumas etc. on the one hand and your domestic cats on the other and compare these primitives with the development that took place on our own planet. In the first place we had no distinction between 'wild' and 'domestic'. We were all cats together.

There was a period in our distant past when we went on all fours, but that did not last for long. We were soon able to stand erect and organize ourselves into 'tribes' (for want of a better word!). However, there were a few similarities; for example, your lions live in prides that are basically matriarchal, the lioness actually being the queen of the jungle rather than the lion the king. The females stand together, caring for each other's young and creating a domestic environment which is secure for their offspring. But the tendency for each pride to allow one or two males to act as both protectors and fathers until they are past their prime, when they are replaced by younger and stronger males who quickly dispose of the young that have been fathered by their predecessors, is one practice in which we never indulged at any period of our history.

Early Paschat tribes worked in much the same way but without the violence. Paschat society was basically matriarchal in that the females took care of the feeding and rearing of the young and ensured that the societal stability essential to the balanced continuance of the tribe was, carried out. Paschats hate disorder of any kind, and you would probably have found Paschat society somewhat restrictive, as everyone knew their place within it from the word `go'. There was, however, a degree of freedom, especially for the young, but one of the things a young Paschat learned from an early age was how to contact his or her transpersonal self and, in so doing, each was able to ascertain his or her karma or blueprint for the life in question. No-one forced these decisions upon them; they simply evolved via the discipline of self-discovery.

Since it fell to the females to keep this order, they were the decision makers, although those decisions were actually carried out by the males. The males were also responsible for physical education and government generally, but always under the intuitive guidance of the females. Neither sex was seen as superior to the other, each carrying out those tasks that were best suited to its talents and physique. Besides, all Paschats knew that they could be born as either male or female, so it didn't really matter in the long run.

In our more primitive times we did tend to think of ourselves as superior to other life forms with which we shared the planet (a stage through which you have been passing for several thousand years), although we were aware that there were certain trees and plants that were more advanced than ourselves, and these we naturally treated with much respect and a great deal of fear, especially during our very primitive stages. Later we came to learn that all life forms are equal in that each contributes something essential to the whole. However, we never went out of our way to attack or persecute those we saw as our inferiors and they were careful to keep their distance from us, although, like your lions, we all drank from the same water hole, metaphorically speaking; that is, each knowing the right time to leave, or stand back for the others.

ANIMAL BEHAVIOURISM:

Much has been written recently concerning the psychology of your domestic pets. It has been suggested by animal behavioural psychologists that it is bad for cats or dogs to be kept in high rise apartments as it is an animal's right to have the freedom to come and go as it pleases, or at least be allowed into the great outdoors for reasonable periods of time. These 'shrinks' as you call them are both right and wrong. They are right in that *all* life forms on Earth, yourselves included, should partake of a degree of outdoor life as appropriate to the climate in which they live, but wrong in that many animals know the kind of environment into which they will be born, or will eventually find themselves, so they do have the choice of selecting a breed that prefers the indoor life. For example, a cat born into a hairless breed such as the Canadian Sphynx or Devon Rex would not care to be cast out into the cold; and the same applies to a lap-dog who prefers his mistress's lap to a set-to in the park with the local canine bully.

'Ah,' you will say, 'but do animal spirits have a choice in the same way that we do?' To which I would reply by repeating the last part of your question – 'in the same way that you do'. Immature essence-fragments exercise little if any control over the bodies they enter, but are simply drawn to them by the compatibility of the soma with their own stage of spiritual development. The more mature the incoming essence-fragment, the more evolved the soma. Your domestic pets therefore fall into roughly the same spiritual categories as yourselves in that there are very young souls that are barely separated from the group-essence, an enormous number of 'middle-of-the-path' essence-fragments and a very few mature souls that are almost ready to move on into faster frequencies (who will no longer need to enter physical bodies on your planet and may even be ready to meet their antiparticles).

The sooner you stop seeing yourselves as some kind of superior race that alone is able to house mature essence-fragments the better. There is many a cat, dog, horse, tree, mineral that houses what I term a mature essence-fragment, but you refer to as an evolved spirit, which is much farther up the evolutionary ladder than a large percentage of your hominid population. Which brings me round to the question of maladjusted pets. Many domestic pets find themselves in environments that are not conducive to their physical or psychological well-being. Cats and dogs react differently to this problem. A dog will often exhibit antisocial behaviour and a degree of violence against humans but, since dogs are essentially pack animals, they will always defer to the 'leader'. In the majority of cases a house-dog will cast its owner in this role, but not necessarily its owner's friends, acquaintances, or anyone its owner might pass in the street! But there again it depends on the nature of the dog. A cat, on the other hand, finding itself in a household with which it is not in harmony, providing it is allowed a degree of freedom, will literally move out and in with someone more agreeable who can cater to its physical and psychological needs. A mistake so often made by human families with young children is to obtain a pet for the children to play with. In many cases this is extremely cruel to the pet, as the majority of you do not raise your progeny from an early age to understand when they are inflicting pain. The pet is also viewed as second-rate to the child or children, which is again a mistake caused by the prevailing climate of hominid insensitivity towards the feelings, sufferings and needs of other species. Pets should not be taken on unless the owners are prepared to grant them equal status to the rest of their family, within their needs, of course. For example, you would not need to cook a three course meal for your dog or cat as you might for your child, but as long as you provide equivalent nourishment for the animal, then that is just and fair.

ANIMAL VIOLENCE:

I have been asked why there is such an increase in pet-violence. The obvious answer is because there has been a corresponding increase in hominid violence. In other words, the energies around and on your planet are accelerating into degeneration and it is the young essence-fragments of *all species* that are the worst affected by this. When questioned recently concerning the increase in canine violence, one of your prominent veterinary surgeons and animal psychologists, Dr. Bruce Fogle, commented: 'Dogs are not capable of spiteful acts. That is a behaviour found only in monkeys and humans. Dogs behave badly, not to get even with their owners or because of a lack of obedience; they do so out of anxiety.' Likewise an anxious cat is not a friendly one and the same applies to other domestic pets favoured in your present day and age. Owners of pets who display violent or unsocial tendencies should look to themselves and not their pets for the cause, like inevitably attracting like! Did Paschats have pets? Of course we did, while in the very early days of our life on the old planet the plant people used to treat our offspring in the same way. But as we advanced, so they withdrew, leaving only the occasional tree as an oracle via which we could communicate with the 'old ones'.

YOUR PRESENT-DAY PSYCHOLOGY:

The evolution of psychology from the work of Freud to the myriad theories that have mushroomed since the nineteen-sixties have proved of great interest to us. Many of these systems are purely exploratory and do not emphasize the need for assertive creativity on the part of the evolving psyche (essencefragment). We also observe a tendency to delve inwards and accentuate the material or Earth ego, which inevitably leads to egocentricity on the one hand and a destructive internal spiralling of energy on the other. Let me explain.

By the cosmic law of non-conservation, all energy should flow outward and it is through the accretions gathered during this circulation that growth is attained, which brings me to address the question of the manifestation of chaos/order at the personal level in the human system, as requested by our Crystal cousins. Since your thoughts contain an energy potential, if you persistently centre these around yourself (introversion) rather than opening them up to the world around you (extraversion) you stand to encourage an imbalance of some kind or other. Any personal energies that are off centre are conducive to chaos within the somatic system, cancer being a typical manifestation of energy inversion. Creative energy that is misplaced because it is thwarted – not allowed the freedom of expression (repressed) – will continue to create and if that creative process is alien to the environment in which it finds itself, then that environment will suffer, be it the human system or any other manifestation of life on your planet or anywhere else in the universe.

The work of the psychologist, or psychiatrist as the case may be, should therefore involve unlocking this energy and teaching the patient or client to send it outwards, for in so doing he or she will find that it is returned with interest and that 'interest' will be of a totally beneficial kind. The holy book upon which you place so much store tells you 'as ye sow so shall ye reap' and exemplifies this principle in a parable about some talents, in which the man who was only given one 'buried it' (held it within himself) rather than multiplying it by investment (projecting it outwards so that it could collect interest – 'accrete' in our terminology). Unfortunately, you tend to take these examples too literally, seeing 'talents' as either units of material exchange or personal abilities.

Many of the new fads that have pervaded the psychology scene over the past two or three decades have been nothing more than mental diversions that could be likened to children playing with bricks. Their efficacy, if indeed they have any, therefore lies in their amusement value but precious little else. Discovering the 'self' may prove highly enlightening to some of you, but I put this question to you: what do you do with it when you have found it? In most cases you take great pride in declaring that you are a 'this' or a 'that'; perhaps you have discovered that your archetype is akin to the nature of a Greek deity such as Artemis, Apollo or Zeus, or an Egyptian divinity like Isis or Horus but, once the glamour wears off and your friends and acquaintances have heard it all, it is soon forgotten and, like the bored child, you seek other areas of entertainment.

We sometimes observe how many so-termed 'spiritual seekers' among you move in butterfly fashion from one fashionable craze to another, always taking but seldom, if ever, dreaming of giving back some of what you have taken from your tutors or lecturers. Likewise, the practitioners of psychology and allied professions often make a good living out of perpetuating these parodies of human observation, providing their clients with a constant flow of dream interpretations and circumspective advice, while also acting out the role of good listeners (dare I say 'sponges'?). Needless to say all this intake does them about as much good as their homilies do for their clients in the long run. A different approach to psychology would benefit both the practitioner and his or her clients; my suggestion would be that the exchange of energies principle would constitute a good basis for a new direction or line of action within that field. Knowing hominids, however, there is always the possibility that there would be some who would go 'over the top' even with this principle, trying to give out more than they actually have; so perhaps you should start with an assessment of what you each have in the first place, which will then give you some idea as to how it should be apportioned during the sending-out process. As your book tells you, some of you are gifted with more energy than others, or your energies may be of a different quality from those of your friends or acquaintances, or even your family.

CHANNELLING AND THE MULTIPLE PERSONALITY SYNDROME:

Channelled communications of the kind we are effecting with Murry at the moment often come under criticism from the professional psychologist or psychiatrist; and not without good reason, I may add, the multiple personality syndrome being among the more easily recognizable mechanisms employed in the psychological compensatory process. Our channel is frequently assessed on these grounds and will be the first to agree that to the metaphysically untutored her efforts would appear to fit that particular bill. But when similar communications from identical communicators are appearing in various parts of the world and among people of vastly different background and qualification that, surely, is stretching even 'the experimenter effect' a little too far. Besides, the multiple personality diagnosis, if applied to every case of mind to mind communication, would imply that no other form of consciousness, including mankind, ever sends thoughts out to anything or anyone else!

Now I do not have to tell you that people, and animals for that matter, in close relationships of any kind, are often able to sense what the other or others are feeling, even when they are separated by time and space. This has been confirmed scientifically in the EPR (Einstein-Podolski-Rosen) paradox. Since the universe contains more intelligences than you (or 1) could ever dream of, it would seem illogical to us Paschats and our Crystal cousins that there should not be some mind-to-mind contact effected, depending, of course, on the compatibility of personality and frequency between the communicator and the recipient. Think about it, but in assessing any such claims be careful that you do not confuse genuine communication with the compensatory mechanisms of mental imbalances since both exist; the dividing line, as in the case of ecstasy/frenzy, is an extremely fine one.

THE NEGOTIATION OF CHAOS:

The negotiation of chaos is another factor that should be taken into consideration by psychologists. There is a little too much emphasis on the damaging effects of stress on the human psychological economy without reference to its character-building properties. A certain amount of stress is essential to human progress since it acts as the spur to personal identity, self-assertion and the realization of the psyche's potential. Chaos is to be encountered at all levels of spiritual ascent. It is only when it becomes out of balance with order, as in the case of your planet, that it is potentially dangerous. Chaotic or solvent energies are essential to the transformative processes that form part of the infinite pattern of life throughout all universes. An over-emphasis on order leads to stagnation, which in turn spawns the seeds of degeneration, while excessive chaos is equally destructive, albeit in a different way. It is therefore essential that both be kept in balance, which lesson is depicted in the symbology of the caduceus where health is concerned and the sistrum for the elemental or cosmic forces. It is interesting to observe that your medical profession have carried the former symbol through to this day, although one wishes they would show it correctly, with the serpents crossing at four places, signifying the fourfold and quarternionic nature of the universe in which you exist. Stylized versions exhibiting one serpent only, or many crossings, dilute or misdirect the energies contained in the symbol and are therefore unhelpful to the healing process.

The usual crop of viruses and germs that invade the human body during childhood are chaotic by nature and yet they generate the antibodies essential to freedom from greater afflictions in later life. Note how those who have avoided a simple complaint like mumps or chicken pox are affected much worse if they contact it during adulthood than they would have been during childhood. Apply the same principle at all levels and you will see quite clearly how the chaos/order balance works.

At the faster frequencies, or higher levels of consciousness as you might call them, chaos and order draw closer and closer, eventually becoming one so that each is contained within the other. However, in certain of the lower frequencies of time's stationery bands, there is a marked separation, resulting in an over-accentuation of either principle; and it is this that renders them both, but chaos in particular, potentially dangerous.

QUESTION: Did you have a system of healing on your old planet and was it anything like that used by the Crystal people?

ANSWER: Of course we had a medical profession just as you have, but it was not as rigid. Our doctors had their basic training, but they also learned psychology side by side with their surgical, anatomical, physiological, herbal and allied studies. In addition to all this, they were also taught to use their extra-sensory powers in combination with the aforementioned. They were not, however, as technologically advanced as their Crystal cousins, but if you want to know about their healing methods you must ask them, as they were certainly different from our own, that is until such times as the two races shared the same planet.

QUESTION: If we want to keep a pet, bearing in mind what you have told us, how can we tell whether we have chosen the right one?

ANSWER: Why not let the pet choose you? Most good breeders will allow their customers to sit well away from a litter of puppies or kittens and so allow one or two of the little ones to make their own approach. Likewise, if you are choosing a pet from an RSPCA, Cats Protection League or Animal Welfare Home, note which animal is drawn to you rather than which one you like the colour, shape or size of. Animals also have the knack of landing on the doorstep of their chosen home. So, if you open your front door one morning and discover that someone has deposited a kitten or puppy there, rest assured that this was no accident, since it evidences the fact that the essence-fragment of that tiny creature was sufficiently powerful to influence the mind of the former owner as to which doorstep to leave it on! Surprised at that? My dear friends, you are influenced *all the time,* in ways you would never believe if I told you and by other intelligences you would for the most part consider to be your inferiors!

QUESTION: Joy Adamson, who, together with her late husband, George, brought an understanding of lions to the public notice with their moving story of the lioness Elsa, apparently believed that she alone was not responsible for her books. In some mystical way, she maintained, Elsa became the force that inspired her. Likewise, I have just read about a clergyman who claims to gain spiritual insight from his dog. There have been other mystics who have learned from humble animals. Is this what you mean when you tell us that some animal spirits are more evolved than we are?

ANSWER: Animal spirits, as you call them, have been guiding mankind from time immemorial. The shamans of old were well aware of this and the many benefits to be gained from a regular dialogue with the spirits of trees, streams, rocks and the Earth herself were well known to them. We find it interesting to note that shamanism is undergoing an extensive revival. While this is excellent in itself, what does worry us is that the new crop of shamans tend to be using methods employed centuries earlier that were designed for the people of their time. Times are different now and heavy drumbeats are not always conducive to the stimulation of the higher chakras, which is what Earth hominids are badly in need of at present. If you are going to pursue the path of primitivism you should divest it of its lower frequencies and address the animal spirits and other communicating intelligences at their more elevated or finer frequencies. Shamans always work with a totem animal, plant, tree, stone etc. Our channel sometimes works in this capacity and guess what her totem animal is? Why, a lion, of course, which follows since she emanated from that evolutionary stream. This does not mean that all shamans originated from the evolutionary streams common to their contacts, but rather tells of a link that goes back in your time and ours, perhaps, with intelligences of other species.

QUESTION: I have heard it said that you can tell a lot about a person from his or her pet, or lack of same. From the point of your understanding of psychology, Mikili, is there any truth in this?

ANSWER: Goodness me, yes. People can also be seen to resemble their pets. The type of person who is exclusively horse or dog orientated is of a quite different psychological make-up to an ardent cat fancier, or a collector of reptiles. Animals have their archetypal affinities, and to discover your archetype will tell you a lot about the animals you like, dislike or fear. Not that I place all that much importance on personal archetypal discovery, but it can help you to piece together a clearer picture of yourself or the people with whom you deal in the course of your everyday life. For example, those who have never kept a pet, have no knowledge of animals and no wish to own (be owned!!!) by one but who, at the same time, would never harm one, are usually totally hominid orientated. This also indicates a close link with the element of water and the emotional system within their psychology so, if you need to appeal to them in any way, you know which bell to ring, so to speak. Horse lovers present yet another group of hominids who are usually earth-orientated and therefore akin to the nature of the spirits of that element, so it would be no use approaching them with a sob-story. There are several categories of dog people ranging from the macho type males who like to be seen with large, ferocious dogs, which they subconsciously or consciously view as symbols of their own egos, to the owners of lap-dogs. Although they would never admit it, most dog owners enjoy being 'head of the pack', even if they only own one hound. I hear your people say: 'You can train a dog to do what you want, make it obedient, have it fall into line, work for *you* as a protector, helper, or simply a good pal who never argues back.' Do I really need to explain this psychology?

While on the subject of dogs, since our home star, Sirius, is in the constellation of Canis Major, some of you have been perplexed as to why we are felines rather than canines. Canis Major is a large galaxy, the stellar energies of which lend experience to many different species including an advanced form of canine life. In fact many of the animals on your planet, especially those that enjoy a close relationship with mankind, have undergone (or are undergoing) evolutionary cycles at one level or another within that constellation. There is, however, an erroneous astrological belief that Sirius exerts a particular influence on Earth canines; in fact Siriun energies affect *all life forms on your planet, but with a specific emphasis on hominids and felines,* and your astrologers would be well advised to revise their teachings accordingly.

Unlike those who tend to favour dogs as pets cat fanciers are a different breed of people altogether. No one ever owns a cat and while some cats may appear to be trainable, they will only submit to such hominid whims if it suits them. Cats cooperate rather than obey, which tends to irritate the more forceful among you who like to rule by will. People who are owned by cats must be prepared for the fact that their pets will ultimately triumph, even if it costs them their lives. They can be 'persuaded', however, but only if it suits their convenience. All this may sound very selfish, a fault not uncommon in young cat essence-fragments. Older cat essence-fragments, however, are capable of the kind of deep devotion usually associated with the ardour of true love. You see they are, like those who worship them, in tune with the element of fire.

Feathered pets range from the family canary or budgie to the fine, keen-eyed birds of falconry. Bird-watchers world-wide often suffer great discomfort in the pursuit of observing the domestic habits of their feathered friends, while the wide open spaces obviously feature strongly in their lives. From a psycho/spiritual viewpoint, those indulging in 'watching', either as a hobby or profession, are reflecting the 'observation mode', bird-watching in particular being symbolic of an evolutionary stage preceding the ascent (flight) of the psyche to a faster frequency. Likewise, the caged bird can symbolize the owner's own 'caged spirit', which will only be freed upon the demise of the soma. Obviously the element of air, with all that that implies, features strongly in the psychology of those people who seek a personal association with the denizens of the airy regions of your planet. Incidentally, should any of our readers be unsure as to which aspects of the human psychology relate to which elements, our channel has covered these in depth in her earlier writings.

People who keep a variety of animals are probably the best balanced in the long run, since it was part of the original blueprint for Earth that all species should live together in harmony. However, we do appreciate that how many and what kind of pets you are able to keep is designated by the kind of economy that prevails on your planet. In simple words, you can or cannot afford it! Now I must hand back to our Crystal friends who would like to tell you a little more about their own background during the period when they, like you, inhabited hominid-type bodies.

Chapter 6

THE CRYSTAL PEOPLE

THE ORIGINS OF THE CRYSTAL PEOPLE:

Several of those who have read *The Lion People* have asked for more information concerning us, the planet we lived on and how we originated. Mikili has already explained to you how certain advanced essence-fragments of another species prepare the way for what is eventually destined to be the dominant life-form on each inhabited planet. Our old planet carried a very strong mineral emphasis which we inherited. It abounded in crystalline structures of great beauty and complexity, like nothing you know on Earth. However, we did not have the lush green forests, green swards and profusion of plant life that clothed the Paschat planet, but rather a fairy-tale-like land of dazzling colour and warmth. Everything about our world was crystal clear and yet soft. The frequencies were extremely fine, as befitted a species that were basically cerebral. Our brains were constructed differently from your own in that the circuits were highly complex and more numerous. The beings who designed our species were intent upon creating a hominid-type genus to the highest degree of refinement, representing the final stage of matter prior to entry into pure energy. Thus we were already well advanced along the evolutionary path before we came to that planet.

COSMIC NURSERIES:

You have heard mention of `cosmic nurseries' in these discourses. Let us define these for you. A cosmic nursery is a young planet which is suitable for the housing of essence-fragments of corresponding youthfulness. Conditions on such planets are usually fairly primitive,

83

requiring manual skills and dexterity for survival. Such essence-fragments live by instinct, their logical and intuitive faculties being as yet undeveloped. All essences shed fragments into nurseries of this kind, although some are able to emerge from them more quickly than others. Our cosmic nursery stage was a very speedy one as compared with some, but now we are talking in linear time which is not really what it is all about. Let us try to put it this way: when an essence shed its fragments throughout time some of those fragments may *appear* to remain in certain time-zones longer than others. Our sojourn on the Crystal planet was, in fact, a fairly short one, whereas the Paschats occupied their planet for a comparatively longer period in inner time. Your Earth was not designed to be a cosmic nursery, but has degenerated into one. As a consequence, the more mature essence-fragments that have become caught up in its evolutionary cycle are very much out of place, their progress impeded drastically, but *only as relevant to one particular pocket of time.* However, this can and does cause considerable frustration to these essence-fragments concerned, which is why so many of your creative geniuses are often ill at ease in their bodies and, as a consequence, their lives appear to assume a chaotic element. Were such spirits to be in their rightful evolutionary position, this suffering would be avoided, as the social and economic conditions would be more conducive to the fostering of their gifts without the pressures encountered within your Earth systems.

But to return to our Crystal experience. One of the tasks that fell to us while we inhabited that planet was to learn how to handle the energies of a collapsing star, which we did; and also to participate in the evacuation of a different species from one planet to another while assisting its members through the painful transformatory process. Once this had been achieved, both we and the Paschats were ready to take our leave of the world of matter as you know it, which is why we are now consciousness manifesting through pure energy.

Old stars shed crystals into space; these are not the diamonds some of your scientists would believe, but atoms of carbon and silicon. Our second Sun was no exception, but the only difference was that we were able to manipulate the whole process.

There are several enigmas concerning the colour of Sirius around the year 2,000 in your time, some Babylonian, Graeco-Roman and mediaeval texts suggesting that it passed through a red stage, while a Chinese record from the Han dynasty (second century BC) also refers to a colour change in Sirius. Of course Sirius appeared as red when our second Sun passed through its red giant stage but, as your scientists so wisely point out, stellar evolution is not so rapid that this transition could have taken place in human history. Interstellar clouds crossing their line of sight to Sirius has been one explanation, but we would like to say that it was caused by an evolutionary transition effected by ourselves *after* we had vacated the Sirius system, the cosmological details of which are too complex for us to convey via the medium of this channel since she does not possess the necessary terms of reference to effect any degree of accuracy. In fact, we would be hard pushed to make ourselves clear to one of your top astronomers at this point in your Earth time.

Our channel is somewhat concerned at this point that we may appear to be taking a high-handed approach with the people of Earth but this is not intended. We ourselves still have a long way to go on our own evolutionary journey so we are not claiming to have all the answers as far as you are concerned. There are, however, a few pointers we can give you and this is what we have tried to do. So please forgive us if at any time we appear to be assuming the professorial role, which is far from our intent.

STRANGE ATTRACTORS:

We have been asked to comment on what your scientists have called 'strange attractors'. First of all it is necessary that we ask our channel to give you the orthodox definition of these phenomena, after which we can add our own observations.
(Strange Attractors, described by the French scientist Professor David Ruelle, who created the phrase):
  'Strange attractors are relevant to the fields of fluid dynamics, chemistry, astronomy, meteorology, and, to some extent, ecology. Think of a point moving in space and staying always in the same region. This region is called an attractor. If the point keeps wandering irregularly on the attractor at all times, then it is called a strange attractor.

  'Strange attractors are used to describe the motions of turbulent fluids in fluid dynamics, and in the study of many other complicated and irregular motions. Applications to meteorology involve attractors of more than three dimensions. These cannot be visualised but can still be handled by computers. Use of strange attractors has improved our understanding of unpredictability in meteorology.'[1]

Your scientists are slowly uncovering a whole new world of phenomena, the significance of which will eventually be seen to extend well beyond the disciplines and fields of research in which they were originally discovered. This applies specifically to strange attractors, fractals and chaos, the latter having already received adequate comment in earlier pages. So let us deal with strange attractors first. As we view these phenomena, they are pockets of energy exhibiting what might at first appear to be chaotic influences but which do, in fact, have a direct bearing on both the matter and unmanifest energy within their jurisdiction. As we have explained to you previously, there is no such thing as an energy pocket that is not ensouled by an intelligence or form of consciousness, and so it is with strange attractors. In your linear years ahead you will learn more about the nature of (and eventually become conversant with) these entities who will, in turn, help you to understand and eventually negotiate those subtle cosmic currents that form some of the conveyor belts for time's energy.

Now let us leave the cosmos and apply strange attractors to you, the reader. Your own lives are frequently affected by the branch of these phenomena that functions within the waveband of the Earth hominid frequencies. For example, many of you may experience situations in which you feel compelled to make decisions that are completely out of character. When viewing these events in hindsight you may wonder how you had the nerve to act in such a rash or unpredictable way. What actually happened was that you encountered a strange attractor, without which energies you would not have accomplished the transformation crucial to your development at that point in your life. Sometimes it becomes necessary for all of us to be shaken out of our routines of complacency and the energies required to effect that much needed, sudden and unpredictable change fall into the 'strange attractor' category. So, when you look back in horror at what you feel to have been stupid or ill-conceived actions, do not be too hard on yourselves, since those decisions and their subsequent outcomes may have been vital to your evolutionary progress at that point in time. And, while it is always advisable to challenge any decisions you might contemplate that could appear to contain a chaotic element, never reject them out of hand. After

---

1 *The Daily Telegraph Science Extra.* Saturday, August 18, 1990.

all, they could emanate from the promptings of a strange attractor. Strange attractors could therefore be viewed as the agencies of chaos on the one hand and the instigators of new beginnings on the other, their specific role in the universal scheme of things being to keep things moving and in so doing avoid stagnation. The ancients of your planet knew about such energies and accorded them a specific emblem which later found its way into the religious symbology of ancient Egypt in the form of the sistrum. Believe us when we tell you that strange attractors exist in every sphere of your visible world, as well as those frequencies with which you are as yet unfamiliar.

FRACTALS:

Now let us look at another word that has come into popular use: fractals. Firstly, we will ask our channel to give you the definition accorded to it by your scientists:
(Fractals are described thus by Professor Benoit Mandelbrot, author of 'The Fractal Geometry of Nature', who gave his name to the Mandelbrot Set):
'Fractals are geometric shapes that are not regular at all, but exhibit about the same degree of irregularity at all scales of examination. That is, an object is a fractal if it looks about the same when exam fined from far away and nearby; if it is 'self-alike'. Coming closer to examine it in greater detail, one finds that small pieces which necessarily seemed from the distance to be formless blobs prove to be well defined objects whose shape is very much the same as that of the previously examined whole.

'This is a property all fractals share with the ferns in which each big branch and each small branch are very much like the whole. But fractals are totally unlike the shapes of Euclid, which are very smooth; as you come closer to a curve in Euclid you see it always become increasingly straight (except of course if you look at a corner, of which there can be only a few).' [1]

We wonder how many observers of these phenomena have noticed that fractals *appear* to work conversely from the normal microcosm/macrocosm sequence? For example, the chaotic states observed in

1 *The Daily Telegraph Science Extra.* Saturday, August 18, 1990.

minute particles, or cell conglomerates, when viewed from afar, display a symmetry of great beauty and purpose. In other words, the sequence is proceeding from chaos to order. Fractals, on the other hand, as your learned adviser has told you 'which necessarily seemed from the distance to be formless blobs, prove to be well defined objects on closer examination...' In other words, we have a kind of inversion of the chaos/order sequence, no?

We would view fractals as part of the geometry of *manifest nature,* or matter at a given frequency, at which they *appear* to exhibit a definition not observable from a distance. Distance can therefore be seen to effect a kind of dissolution for, although the shape of the fractal holds good when viewed from afar, its definition is blurred. Might we not use as an analogy a beam of light which diffuses as it spreads out? In other words, the energy of the fractal, like that of the light, receives its strongest *focus* at the point at which it is more clearly defined? So what we are dealing with is the *matter to energy sequence in reverse* which hints at an unsuspected aspect of computer development, while also serving as a clear indication that time's arrow is *not* limited to the forward direction only.

QUANTUM MECHANICS:

Here is another study that is proving to be an excellent stepping stone from your physical sciences to those frequencies that are faster, finer and therefore less easily defined in purely physical terms. Once again we ask our channel to give you the accepted definition:
(Quantum Mechanics is described by Professor David Bohm of Birkbeck College, London, who is currently researching interpretations of this field thus):
'The essential feature of quantum mechanics is that energy and other properties come in discrete packets. The quantum was discovered earlier this century, demonstrating that particles moved in definite jumps with definite amounts of energy, an advance on Newtonian mechanics [the fundamental laws that describe the motion of most objects in the universe] where particles move continuously. Quantum mechanics is now a basic law in physics with applications in anything from solids to radiation.'[1]

---

1 *The Daily Telegraph Science Extra.* Saturday, August 18,1990.

What we like best in this definition is the reference to quantum jumps, about which much has already been said in this book while there is still more to come (our channel permitting!). Why some scientists should confine the phenomenon of the quantum jump, or leap, to the subatomic worlds mystifies us somewhat, since whatever happens at one level also occurs at every other, both in what you would probably refer to as 'above' and 'below' but which we prefer to see in terms of quality or density of frequency.

As your knowledge of quantum mechanics grows, it will have the effect of creating a chasm within your scientific establishment, since the only logical conclusion to be drawn from its study is a metaphysical one, which will not be acceptable to many die-hard materialists. For those of our readers who would like to know more about how the quantum worlds relate to your everyday life, your paranormal experiences and your beliefs in the after-life, may we recommend you to read *Time: The Ultimate Energy* which was written by our channel through a combination of her own studies/ research and a little help from our leonine cousins and ourselves!

Our channel is displaying symptoms of anxiety and fears that she might not be conveying the more technical side of our message correctly. But we are reasonably satisfied with her interpretations of our cerebral impulses so far, although, of course, in all of these studies we are barely scratching the surface of the corpus of knowledge that still remains to be resurrected in your earthly science. We are therefore obliged to limit our instructions to the amount she can absorb and rationalize on the one hand, and that for which your own scientists have provided a few useful terms of reference on the other.

THE GENOME PROJECT:

There has been much debate between scientists, philosophers, religious adherents and laypersons concerning the proposed genome project, and our views have been sought. Once again we ask our channel to effect the definitions accepted by your scientific profession (there are quite a few for this one!):

(This information is given by James D. Watson, an American molecular biologist who, working in Britain in 1953 with Francis Crick, Maurice Wilkins and the late Rosalind Franklin, discovered

the structure of DNA, the chemical which carries the code for all hereditary characteristics. The three men were awarded the Nobel Prize for Medicine in 1962)

'DNA: deoxyribonucleic acid, the fundamental chemical of inheritance which carries the genetic blueprints (or genes) that determine how we are built.

GENE: the smallest unit of heredity made of DNA.

GENOME: the genetic apparatus of an animal or plant considered as a whole and characteristic of it.

RNA: ribonucleic acid; with DNA one of two classes of genetic material. RNA is usually a single strand, unlike DNA.

GENETIC ENGINEERING: the technology of manipulating genes by cutting them out, growing them in culture and inserting them into other cells or living things.

NUCLEIC ACID: vital to all living organisms as carrier of genetic information.

NUCLEOTIDE: compound that symbolizes a distinct part of the genetic code.

RECOMBINANT DNA: DNA from one source joined to DNA from another.[1]

Well! What can we say! It must sound all very technical to many of our readers. But, take heart, it has the same effect on us, your commentators! The question of genetic engineering has already been covered in earlier chapters, so all that remains is for us to say our piece regarding the genome project. It will be brief and here it is: your geneticists will be in for a few surprises in that they will discover certain information that will serve to effect distinct categories between:

(a) different psychological types
(b) hereditary knowledge, gifts and talents
(c) psi abilities and pre-birth 'memories'
(d) 'mystery' genes.

The imprint of the latter is present in the DNA and may initially give rise to some problems of interpretation. You see, your cosmic roots are also present in your DNA, so the essence-fragment that is Professor Fred Hoyle may yet have cause to rejoice when certain of his theories are proved to be correct. However, this project will take a long time

---

1 *The Daily Telegraph Science Extra.* Saturday, August 18, 1990.

to complete and there will be a point in your future at which it will be violently interrupted ... And thereby we rest our case!

THE ELECTROMAGNETIC NATURE OF LIFE:

There has been much debating among your scientific community regarding what is referred to as a great unified theory (GUT), in which all the accepted energy sources – gravity, electromagnetic and nuclear, in their various potencies – dissolve into a single point of power (see *Time: The Ultimate Energy,* pp. 15-17). All life is, in fact, a manifestation of light, but in a far more practical way than the esotericists would imagine. Light has an excitatory effect on electrons, bringing them into a high energy state, which is both absorbed by each life-form and then passed on until a cycle is complete and the energy is spent. Since electromagnetism appears to produce such a pronounced effect, it could be viewed as one of the dominant connecting energy-threads between all life operating within the waveband of your material universe. Your own scientists have observed that organisms only maintain their structure by the constant dissipation of metabolic energy, which has suggested to them that an organism is perhaps more of a process or happening than an object. Translate this into human terms and the picture of your life's experiences takes on a new meaning. However, centuries of faulty programming regarding the death syndrome is hardly conducive to an in-depth understanding of this state of transition.

But let us return to the subject of electromagnetic fields. Having established that all organisms, including yourselves, are influenced by these energies, to what extent are your cerebral mechanisms conscious of this and how do they respond? Neural sensitivity varies with each person, but there is a rule which may not have made itself obvious to your researchers at present which is: tolerance to radioactivity goes hand in hand with extreme sensitivity to electromagnetic fields. So, while all life is subject to the influences of the GUT (see above) energies proposed by your scientists, how each individual unit that carries the life-force responds to those energies will be an individual thing, decided by its stage of cosmic maturity. Mature essence-fragments (old souls) eventually reach the stage where they are actually able to manipulate pure energy, although during the lead-up to the acquisition of this facility they pass through several interesting stages, some of which appear to produce valid results and others not. This is simply due to faulty handling of the techniques involved and should not be taken as a rejection from 'on high', 'the gods', or whichever role the individual has chosen for the supreme creative force. And one other point, your GUT is not complete; there is another important energy source in the universe which you have still to discover, aside from how to use your minds, that is!

We have drawn our channel's attention to an article in a scientific magazine from which we would like her to quote, so that we may follow with appropriate comment:

'Living systems are by their very nature neither subjects alone, nor objects isolated, but both subjects and objects in a mutually communicating (and defining) universe of meaning. In a very deep way, each living being is implicated in every other. Each suffering, each extinction affects us and impoverishes us. Similarly we partake of the joy and creativity of each individual organism. The capacity of organisms to evolve thus depends on their capacity for communication.

'... In addition to phase stability, a coherent electromagnetic field has the paradoxical property of factorizability. This means that although the parts maintain a coherent pattern as a whole, they still behave statistically independently of one another. Thus coherence does not imply uniformity, or that every individual part of the system is necessarily doing the same thing all the time. An intuitive way of thinking about it is in terms of a grand symphony, or rather a jazz band in which individuals are doing different things and yet are in tune and in step with the whole. It is a state of effortless cooperativity in which individuals cooperate simply by doing their own thing and expressing themselves... the trend in evolution is towards emergence of organisms with longer and longer life-spans and finally in the case of social organisms and human beings we see the emergence of social traditions that span many generations. The link with social tradition is the clue to the meaning of this energy flow through a coherent field of ever increasing bandwidth. Electromagnetic signals of different frequencies are involved in communication within and between organisms, and between organisms and the environment. The coherent platform is a prerequisite for universal communication.'[1]

1 *On the Coherent Lightness of Being,* Mae-Wan Ho and Fritz-Albert Popp. *CADUCEUS.* Issue no. 13,1991.

The scientists from the International Institute of Biophysics who wrote those words are quite correct. And we hope that, in the light of the aforegoing, it will become blatantly obvious that if mankind is persistently unable to communicate with the other life forms with which it shares your planet and with the life-giving intelligences in the cosmos as a whole, it will not survive in this physical system. As we view your Earth at the moment, there are precious few among you who are even prepared to acknowledge the fact that other life-forms, from the most minute to the largest, carry both an energy quotient and a degree of consciousness! If we are sounding judgmental we apologize, for this is not our intention. What we are trying to do is to warn you that, if you persist along the road to self-destruction, the consequences will be horrendous beyond your imagination.

THE FUTURE OF GAIA:

After reading the above your next question will more than likely be 'what are these horrendous consequences?' Our channel (at ours and the Paschats' instigation) has been trying to bring certain future events to the public eye for many years now. But the time in your Earth years is becoming increasingly shorter. Without going into too many of the gory details (your science fiction writers and film makers seem to have made a good job of this already) your planet will experience a pole shift, or axis tilt if you prefer. This will have the effect of changing your climate completely, since Gaia will move slightly nearer to her parent star. As a result, there will be considerably less habitable land available and, consequently, a very *much* smaller world population. As she turns to change her position, the oceans will adjust accordingly, covering many lands that are now above water and exposing others that are at present resting beneath the waves. Of the lands that survive, those that are at present hot will become extremely cold, while your present arctic and antarctic regions will once again be exposed to subtropical temperatures (we assure you that they have been so in the past!). Many of your great industrial nations will cease to exist and with them to the bottom of the oceans will go their 'satanic mills', as your mystical poet so aptly described them; also much of the other paraphernalia of your so-termed 'civilized world'.

Of course there will be survivors, but these will be a new breed of hominids who are the rightful custodians of the body of Gaia. How these selected survivals are likely to take place is, however, our secret and will remain so until the time is right for us to issue appropriate instructions and warnings. I hear our channel thinking 'goodness me, isn't this all a little bit too sci-fi for a book of this kind?' We are sorry, little Paschat, but the time is becoming too short for the niceties of current hominid conventions and, therefore, what has to be said *has to be said.* If it is of any comfort to you, little cousin, you will be finally returning to your own kind, so please do not worry too much about reproducing our message in print.

QUESTION: You state you are now beings of pure energy, who have long since left behind the 'nuts and bolts' stage of technological development. This being the case, why your interest in the scientific research that is going on here at present?

ANSWER: Because one of the tasks that has fallen to us is to help your researchers to bridge the gap between the physical sciences and the new metaphysics that must and will become a feature in your future. In fact, beings from our own race have incarnated among you for this specific purpose. The division between the physical sciences and metaphysics is a false one and should *not* exist. The barrier therefore needs to be broken down and, since your scientists are so conditioned into the reality of the physical worlds only, an injection of mature essence-fragments who will naturally reject that kind of programming has become essential in order that the transition can be effected as smoothly and painlessly as possible.

Perhaps this is as good a place as any to make one thing quite clear: we make no claims whatsoever to possessing an all-embracing knowledge of the universe, or that ultimate creative state that you call God. We, like yourselves, are only on one particular rung of the celestial ladder, albeit a few steps higher, but still an infinity away from the top; nor do we know of or have communication with any genuine beingnesses or intelligences who claim that privilege. We simply learn from those who teach us as we in turn teach you. This does not preclude us, of course, from addressing our respects to the highest source *we can conceive of,* in the same way that you pray to your particular concept of the supreme or ultimate creative force.

When our task with you is completed, we and the Paschats will leave your dimension to assume other cosmic duties. There will be those of our kind among you who will leave with us, after which their experiences in Earth hominid bodies will assume the quality of some past dream that has, however, left an indelible mark on their own essence-consciousness and that of the group essence to which they belong.

Suggested reading:

The Reversing Earth by Peter Warlow. (J. M. Dent & Sons)
Pole Shift by John White. (A.R.E. Press, Virginia Press, Virginia, USA)
Gaia and the Evolution of Coherence, Fritz-Albert Popp and Mae-Wan Ho. (International Institute of Biophysics, Technology Centre, Opelstrasse1O, 6750 Kaiserlautern 25, Germany; and Developmental Dynamics Research Group, Open University, Walton Hall, Milton Keynes, MK7 6AA, U.K.)

Chapter 7

KAINI AND THE CRYSTAL PEOPLE

KAINI

ON SHAMANISM:

It is me again, dear things, with what I hope will be a few helpful comments on your current trends in spiritual seeking, which involve delving into the past for answers to the enigmas of modern-day life. My first port of call will be the office of shaman, which certainly appears to be enjoying a revival in certain of your cultures. This naturally bodes well for those energies and conscious entities who have suffered rejection and separation from their hominid brothers, a rift sadly due to the extraordinary attitudes adopted by some of your major world religions on the one hand and the exaggerated materialistic stance resulting from left-brain addiction on the other. Shamanism may certainly be seen to present an excellent gateway to animism and the mineral, plant and animal kingdoms but, cosy and friendly as it may appear at first glance, it has its pitfalls.

As has already been mentioned to you earlier in these dialogues, the shamanic accoutrements that were valid centuries earlier do not necessarily apply today. The psychological effects of certain drum-beats, for example, are known to produce ASCs (altered states of consciousness) which, while they may *appear* evidential to those who experience them, amount to absolutely nothing as far as evolution, spiritual progress and cosmic understanding are concerned. But, rather, they have the effect of taking you back in time to a period in the history of your race which is best left behind. I am sure some of you will be quick to point out to me that, since all time is one, the past and future are also one, which is basically true, but not in quite the same way as you may see it. You see, repetitive experience is both worthless and against cosmic law. Only if that experience varies, even slightly, is it valuable to the overall evolutionary plan. An essence-fragment incarnating into, shall we say, a native American Indian tribe six thousand years ago would demand an entirely different set of experiences from another fragment from that same essence entering life in your present day and age. By all means seek wisdom from the past, but evaluate the lessons learned in the light of your experiences in the *now*.

The true value of shamanism lies in the ability of the shaman to contact other life-forms and intelligences, some obvious, others not so obvious, with whom you share the body of Gaia. Drum-beats, rattles and the other paraphernalia of shamanism are not essential to its efficient functioning as a valid system of spiritual awareness and enlightenment. In fact, as we have already mentioned, certain rhythms are noted for stimulating the lower chakras and goodness knows that is something hominids most certainly do NOT need. Your mass media appears to go over the top on this issue, while many of your fiction writers also specialize in catering for the less desirable aspects of the hominid psychology. Were your planet on its correct evolutionary course, the sensations of your lower chakras would have been worked through centuries ago and long since forgotten and your species would now be experiencing through the Visuddhu (throat) and Ajna (pineal or 'third eye') chakras.

QUESTION: While you are on the subject of shamans and medicine men, could you please tell us something about the legends of the Hopi Indians, who seem to know an awful lot about Sirius. I believe they also claim to have had divine ancestors. Is this true?

ANSWER: Hopi Indian traditions have certainly come to the forefront in recent years. But then, so have several other systems from ancient cultures whose traditions tell of divine ancestors, or beings from the stars. The Hopi Indians claim that a clan of non-humans they refer to as the Kachina people guided them to their present lands in Arizona and imparted a great deal of knowledge, both practical and esoteric, to them before they eventually left to return to their own world. I will ask Murry to quote from a book about Hopi traditions written by an anthropologist:

> 'The Kachina people did not come to the Fourth World like the rest of the people. *In fact, they were not people. They* were spirits sent to give help and guidance to the clans, taking the forms of ordinary people and being commonly regarded as the Kachina Clan.'[1]

1 *Alien Intelligence,* Stuart Hotroyd. Page 62.

97

According to the information given to the Hopis by the Kachinas, the human race inhabited three other planetary worlds before it came to your present planet and it is destined to move on to other worlds in the future in order to further its evolution. The Hopis believe that the Kachinas came from Sirius (see *THE LION PEOPLE*) and they celebrate religious and secular ceremonies commemorating their arrival and departure to this day.

Now, dear things, you will naturally want to know whether these beings were from outer space or some highly civilized race that existed in prehistoric times. The above text actually answers your question for you *'...taking the forms of ordinary people...'* Much as I would like to tell you that they were, these gentle people were not from outer space, but from a civilization that had been seeded by divine ancestors, and it was this doctrine that they taught to the Hopis. There are similar myths and legends in many parts of your planet, most of which originated from the same two sources, one of which was Pacific based and the other associated with a land that once occupied a position in the Atlantic ocean. If you examine some of these myths carefully, you will soon be able to distinguish one source from the other, the former carrying serpentine and reptilian undertones and the latter hints of leonids and beautiful hominids.

While touching briefly on the early reptilian influence on your planet, I wonder how many of you have connected the *thalamus,* which some of your scientists refer to as the `old brain', or `reptilian brain', with matters we discussed earlier in this book? I will leave you all to work that one out.

QUESTION: Kaini, you appear to place a lot of importance on mythology. Could you please tell us if there is any scientific significance behind two particular myths. The first is the story of Semele and the second the story of Aphrodite and Anchises.

ANSWER: I gather you are referring to the danger involved in the abrupt frequency changes indicated in both of these stories?

QUESTION: That's it exactly, how did you guess?

ANSWER: We leonids have been known to indulge in more than a smidgin of telepathy at times (ha ha ha). But, seriously, of course you are correct and I will try to explain it to you. For the benefit of any readers who might not be familiar with either of these tales from Greek mythology, I must needs ask Murry to give you a short resume of what happened.

The Semele Myth:

Semele, daughter of King Cadmus of Thebes, caught the eye of the amorous Zeus – father of the Gods – and a love affair ensued. Zeus's wife, Hera, heard of the affair and, being a very jealous lady, decided to nip it in the bud. She therefore disguised herself as a nurse and slyly suggested to Semele that she request her love to appear to her in his full Olympian glory (knowing full well that Semele would be destroyed by such a manifestation), for how else could she be sure that he was not, in fact, some terrible immortal monster in disguise? In a moment of passion Zeus had promised Semele that he would grant her whatever she asked, but when she put Hera's suggestion to him, knowing what the outcome would be, he begged her to reconsider her request. Semele, however, was adamant and, since Zeus's promise had been overheard by the other Olympians, he was obliged to display his full radiance. Being unable to endure such dazzling fire Semele was immediately consumed and the child she carried in her womb would also have perished were it not for a thick shoot of ivy, which miraculously created a green screen between the unborn babe and the celestial fire of Zeus.

KAINI:

Now isn't that a lovely story? And so meaningful. In case, dear things, you had not already put two and two together let us analyse it in the cosmological and evolutionary context. Zeus represents not a single man or god, but a highly evolved race entrusted with the task of bringing a particular genetic strain from one frequency to another, Semele representing the slower or lesser evolved state. The Hera character is purely the catalyst since she comes from the same world (Olympus) as Zeus. The world from which Zeus and his family hail is more radioactive, or of a different electromagnetic frequency, perhaps (I am having difficulty with terms of reference for this one!), the nature of which has a quickening effect on the kind of physical matter manifest at Semele's level which, shall

99

we say, corresponds with your own. I will try to put this into the scientific context for you and say that certain energies that exist in dimensions or wavebands of faster frequencies would have the effect of accelerating entropy, so that they would automatically precipitate the imminent collapse of any matter from a lower band that they might come into contact with.

By now you must have realized that the myth is alluding to your own planet, the 'green' reference being obvious. Certain chemicals emitted from the plant kingdoms (trees in particular) help to create an eco-system that is conducive to your own kind of hominid habitation, while also accommodating other life-forms appropriate to the evolutionary pattern of the overall ecosystem. Dionysus is, of course, mankind and his later exploits, periods of madness, and eventual return to sanity through his own efforts and the tutorship of the satyr Silenus (right brain hemisphere), note the whole of his evolutionary progress from its shaky beginnings to his eventual acceptance among the gods of Olympus (final ascent to the next dimension). I would suggest that our readers consult this myth for the full details of Dionysus, for in so doing they may learn something about themselves. He was, of course, 'twice-born', which in itself says much!

The second myth referred to by our worthy questioner concerns the Greek goddess of love, Aphrodite. (What a blessing we Paschats made it our business to study your mythology before embarking on our teaching programme!) Once again I will ask Murry to tell the tale:

Aphrodite and Anchises:

> As a punishment for distracting his divine mind, Zeus caused the goddess Aphrodite to fall blindly in love with a mortal man, the Trojan shepherd Anchises, whose beauty rivalled that of the gods. After a blissful night spent together Aphrodite appeared to Anchises in all her divine splendour. Being fully aware that any man who has lain with an immortal goddess would be stricken with premature old age, the shepherd was filled with terror. But Aphrodite reassured him and promised him a godlike son, asking him only that the name of the child's mother would never be revealed. The child was the pious Aeneas, later venerated as the founder of Rome.

KAINI:

Are we left supposing that Anchises did pass on quickly from premature old age? Obviously, since his son founded a new dynasty (Rome) following the eventual demise of the old one (classical Greece). Here we have the 'sons of god and daughters of men' theme in reverse, the human male being the recipient of attentions from another dimension. His progeny was, however, mortal, in spite of its maternal associations, but then there is always the gene to consider and Aeneas obviously inherited this. But surely it is the premature old age reference that our questioner is referring to. I do not think I need to explain this further as I have already covered it above. But suffice it to say that physical cohabitation between species of differing densities (faster frequencies are always less dense than slower ones) would inevitably result in the hasty demise of one of the parties. If you care to look back to the closing era. of your World War 2 you will observe how your own meagre attempts at generating radioactivity for adverse purposes resulted in some pretty ghastly mutations. The subject of the mutatory effects of radiation and precipitation in alien electromagnetic bands has already been covered by our Crystal cousins, so I would refer our dear questioner back to their earlier comments on the subject.

As you have no doubt gathered there is a cosmological, scientific and psychological explanation behind all of your myths, from the common fairy tales you read to your progeny to the more complex classical offerings of

Homer and Hesiod who were, after all, only repeating (albeit in more poetic form) tales that had been told to them. Might I suggest that you view all your myths in this context, which will save my having to bore my readers with tales they can easily look up in their libraries, and also alleviate the need for me to deal with any further questions on your mythologies.
Thank you.

QUESTION: Could you tell us anything about high frequency vibrational medicine? We have been reading a book of what we assume to be channelled teachings, and mention of this particular subject aroused our curiosity.

ANSWER: Commenting on other channellings always presents a problem since you are all individuals and, as we have previously explained, communicating entities are limited to the vocabulary and terms of reference available in the cerebral programming of the channeller. The specific connection to which you refer is known to us, however, but it is not our policy to pass judgement on the efforts of others. Suffice it to say that the approach used would not be one that we would employ, and we plead innocent of any involvement in the 'revelations' concerned!

There was, however, at one time in the Crystal people's past, a therapy that might broadly fit that description, about which they could tell you more than we Paschats. So I will hand over to them.

THE CRYSTAL PEOPLE:

The question of high frequency vibrational medicine has been referred to us by Kaini. Let us first of all sort out the words in use here. High frequency we can accept. Vibrational, also. But medicine? We fear this word might convey an erroneous impression of the procedures we employed in our evolutionary youth. What we did was this: we erected a biogram of the personal sonic and genetic codes of the individual concerned, a kind of geometrical paradigm, if you like, which represented that individual in a perfect state of health and balance. When any form of imbalance was experienced, or in your language that person became ill, another reading was taken which naturally differed slightly from the original. Each reading was fed into a separate 'computer' (for want of a better word, but rest assured these bore no resemblance to your present technological gadgetry). This apparatus took the form of two upright poles placed apart, each of which threw the respective reading into relief on a visual display unit at the upper end. The reading given for the sick state of the patient was then transferred via a 'beam' to the pole containing the balanced reading, one being placed over the other so that the obvious discrepancies were in full view. Here we come to the technical difficulties, as the kind of energy used was not strictly vibrational according to your understanding of the word, but an amalgam of sound and light. The pole containing the double biogram was then energized by this 'force', which had the effect of adjusting the 'sick' reading to the contours of the 'whole' biogram, thus effecting a complete healing. Nor was there any need for that person to be present, although in the early days of our experimentation with this method we did connect the sick person directly to the apparatus and the energy used was purely sonic. We later dispensed with this and similar procedures and worked from mind to mind and mind to matter. By the end of our evolutionary cycle, however, there was no gadgetry or machinery of any description on our planet as there was no need for it.

QUESTION: Will we on Earth have to go through the nuts and bolts stage in these things before we reach the pure mind-power state?

ANSWER: As far as we see, your evolution will proceed somewhat differently, mind-power and technology developing side by side. The reason for this is that your species has a lot of catching up to do which will require a condensing of experience over a comparatively short period of your time. Eventually, however, your own age of the machine will come to an end and such impedimenta will provide interest and amusement as museum pieces to future generations of Earthlings.

QUESTION: Does that mean that the world is not going to end when the poles shift and that some of us will be saved?

ANSWER: Of course, although, as has already been explained to you, after the Earth's axial position is altered the climate will change so drastically that the number of habitable parts will have decreased considerably. As a result, there will be far fewer people on your planet, which is how it should have been in the first place, since your Earth was not designed to accommodate such a multitude of your species. Let us look at it this way: a mother gives birth to four children with whom she is able to cope adequately, providing them with all the necessities for their growth, strength and happiness. But then fifty more children are suddenly thrust upon her and, try as she may, she has neither the resources nor the physical and mental strength to cope with them. To make matters worse, they are an unruly brood, quite unlike her own progeny whose lives they proceed to make a misery. Worn to a frazzle and with her own children starving and needy, the mother sends out a desperate plea for help to her sisters and brothers who live some distance away. The call is heard and her relatives decide on a suitable plan of action. That, in a nutshell, is what has happened on your Earth.

QUESTION: This is all very worrying. Please tell us, who are these intruders and why are they allowed to come here and destroy our beautiful planet?

ANSWER: Young man, how do you know that you are not one of them? It so happens that you are not, your very concern for Gaia speaking for itself. We understand Kaini and Mikili have already tried to explain to you what occurred during the early days of your planet's evolutionary cycle, but we will qualify it further if you wish and, perhaps, add another slant to the tale. The intrusion of the cosmic virus about which you have already been told had the effect of slowing down the evolutionary progress of the planet itself and all beings living thereon. This tended to inhibit the entry of mature essence-fragments and attract very young essence-fragments, or souls as you call them, who should not be with you at all but in some cosmic nursery. Because immature essence-fragments are naturally more physically orientated than older souls, they usually find it easy to overcome the latter and rule by force of arms, belligerence and competition not forming part of the experiences of mature essence-fragments, particularly during the latter stages of their evolutionary cycle just prior to' 'ascending' to a non-physical dimension. (We have used the word 'ascending' here as we feel it conveys more of what we are trying to tell you than referring to a change to a faster frequency, but both are, in fact, the same.)

Perhaps a few explanations of how cosmic maturity, or soul age, manifests on a planet like your own might help you to work out for yourselves who are and who are not Gaia's real children. But a word of warning here, as this is why we have hesitated to bring this information into the picture before: because you are native to your planet and a true child of Gaia does NOT automatically make you better than those who are not, but simply older. Within a true cosmic family, the older children do not look down on their younger brothers and sisters and treat them with disdain because they attend a different school. Within the home (cosmos) all are 'family' and it is only during school hours, or 'term-time' as you call it, that there is a separation.

IMMATURE ESSENCE-FRAGMENTS *(Young Souls):*

These are usually self-orientated, their interests centering around physical pleasures, acquisition, competition and practical prowess.

Such people often excel at sport, have great stamina and a deep sense of racial identity. Immature essence-fragments always respect physical strength, despise weakness and are naturally attracted to those they feel to be strong and powerful in any walk of life. As they live very much on the surface, they are seldom drawn to deeper considerations, although there are sometimes those among them who are highly dexterous, showing a marked aptitude for certain of the more practical left-brain talents or skills. They are inevitably drawn to group situations and noise and are seldom able to face silence. Being easily manipulated via their emotions renders them vulnerable to the machinations of the type of charismatic world leaders that have tended to dominate your Piscean age. The bulk of the followers of the major world religions is comprised of young souls who are disinclined to think for themselves, preferring to follow established codes of ethics and belief.

MEDIUM AGED FRAGMENTS *(Souls who have passed the stage of cosmic childhood but have not yet attained to the wisdom and awareness of cosmic maturity):*

This category does include some of Gaia's children, although it also accommodates quite a few souls that are alien to her body; and we do not mean star-beings who are with you temporarily to help out. These mid-way souls may be recognized by their desire to intellectualize everything, their leftbrain being decidedly more active than their right brain, which will render them good at intelligence tests (which we view as utterly worthless and certainly not a valid method of assessing either soul-age or creative gifts). They deal only in material facts and show a subconscious fear of anything they cannot relate to the physical world. This is because they are unconsciously aware of the power of their right-brain but, like the young person who keeps his or her distance when catching sight of the expert who is handling some highly volatile substance, they eschew older souls who are more right-brain orientated, labelling them 'cranks' or 'misfits'.

We have observed with interest how those who excel in certain of your more physically orientated sciences are lauded as 'experts' when they carry off some treasured accolade or are granted laureate status but, should they stray for one moment from the established ways of thinking, their past efforts are conveniently forgotten and they are spoken of in hushed tones as having 'gone off the rails a bit'. The same applies to your philosophers and here Plato springs to mind. Those of his writings that fit in with the beliefs currently espoused by your academic establishment are fully accepted and understood. But, in daring to suggest that there might have been a civilization that was more knowledgeable and scientifically advanced prior to your own, the great philosopher is accused of having deviated from sanity, suffered a brainstorm, or at best fabricated it all as an amusing pastime!

Most mid-way souls, however, are caring, considerate and loyal. They may not rise to great heights of transcendental perception, but their predisposition towards order rather than chaos, which they usually endeavour to express in the only avenues available to them in modem society, is laudable. Their task in a truly balanced society, such as should exist on your planet at present but, sadly, does not, would be to foster and protect the mature essence-fragments, who are their natural teachers and spiritual leaders, so that they in turn will receive (or are receiving if you can conceive of the 'all time is one' concept, which in fact it is) similar courtesies in their mature mode in another timezone.

MATURE ESSENCE-FRAGMENTS *(Old Souls):*

Do not be deceived into thinking that the propensity for psychism is automatically a hallmark of this group. Psychism can manifest through any cosmic age-group, as can psycho-kinetic energy. We would describe the mature soul as being 'more aware'; aware of the life-force in all things, aware of their place in the universe, of their cosmic roots, of the turmoil that Gaia is at present experiencing and of the imbalances that dominate your planet. Mature essence-fragments are not by nature belligerent or competitive, which means that they are seldom, if ever, to be found among the rich or materially successful. They do occasionally come before the public eye, but usually in some philanthropic or philosophically controversial way. Young souls seldom target them, but they do tend to 'needle' the middle group, especially when they fail to conform to the current modes of thinking and intellectualizing that are generally accepted by your popular collectives. In other words, a 'norm' is established, which more or less suits both the young and middle groups, but frequently fails to accommodate more mature essence-fragments. However, it would be a mistake to assume that this category is comprised of drop-outs; quite the contrary, in fact, as self-discipline is one of the hallmarks of the mature essence-fragment. Such old souls are to be found among the 'serving' professions, doctors, social workers, counsellers, therapists, artists, musicians, nurses, gardeners and so forth. Old souls seldom attach themselves to large religious or any other collective, for that matter, as they have reached that stage of understanding where they know that the only way to go is alone, but with love in their hearts for every *thing* else, for they are by nature animists! Being aware of the life-force in everything they will naturally treat all things, animals, plants, trees, minerals, all life-forms, in fact, with respect.

One final comment: among highly advanced species, differences between the sexes are considerably less pronounced to the point of being unrecognizable; the more evolved the group essence the closer its members are to that spiritual androgyny that defines the truly cosmically mature. This applies not only to appearances but also to attitudes, needs, and the emphasis placed on what you refer to as 'libido' which, we do assure you, is at its most active *during extreme cosmic (or spiritual) youth!*

THE ATTITUDE OF THE VARIOUS SOUL-AGE GROUPS TO THE ANIMAL KINGDOMS:

Young souls will often view an animal as something over which they can exercise a degree of power, or alternatively as an amusement for their own young which may or may not work out for the unfortunate animals depending on the soul-age of the human young concerned. They therefore tend to dislike animals that do not bend to their will, or perform for their amusement when called upon to so do. Medium souls are often status-conscious where animals are concerned; observe how certain members of your designated 'classes' (be those classes designated financial or hereditary) always favour certain breeds of dog, to keep a cat other than for farming purposes, for example, not being at all befitting someone of their background. More eccentric medium souls often favour the kind of unusual pets that are rarely comfortable in the environment offered to them and, consequently, seldom live very long lives in their imprisonment. Mature essence-fragments are usually very much at home with both the animal and plant kingdoms and will tend to treat all things as equal with themselves, sharing their homes, tables and sleeping places with those they love, no matter what their species. A lot has already been said concerning animals earlier in this book, so we will stop at this point.

A CLASSLESS SOCIETY?

We have heard many of you, who consider yourselves to be cosmically mature, speaking or writing about the equality of the new age which will indeed be the age of the individual. But there are traps into which this kind of thinking can take you, so let us see what they are and in so doing be prepared. There is a correct design for material life according to balanced cosmic standards which we and the Paschats observed during our evolutionary journey and which is also observed in many other parts of the universe where the balance between order and chaos is closely sought after. In this design, each person serves according to (a) his or her stage of cosmic maturity; and (b) the physical make-up and specific talents of the particular essence-fragment concerned. The physically strong person would therefore attend to those tasks that demand physical strength, the mentally endowed would concern themselves with matters appropriate to their abilities and the old souls would go about their tasks of instructing and broadening the cosmic awareness in both other groups. This system would demand that wisdom was accorded more credence and those dispensing it were not required to indulge in heavier physical or complicated mental tasks. In your terms of reference, we are talking of a sacerdotally ruled society, which would be totally unacceptable to you in your present stage of thinking. But this is understandable, since you have come to associate wisdom or 'spirituality' with religion, when the two are by no means synonymous. So you will go on requiring those with creative minds and wisdom to carry out tasks for which they are totally unsuited in order to meet the economic demands of your modern society; and you will continue to look amazed when they choose an appropriate exit door through which to flee from their torment!

'What, then, is the answer? Is it complete equality? Believe us when we tell you there is no such thing in the universe. There is mutual respect, love, caring and acknowledgement of the gifts or talents of others but, since you are each unique individuals with your own personal cosmic blueprint, how can you all be equal?

Complementary, yes. Equal, no. The truly mature essencefragment, who has experienced cosmic individuation, is able to accept all others on complementary rather than equal terms if you can see the difference; and in so doing is able to effect a perfect harmony with every thing and every being around themselves, both in the seen and unseen worlds. You may indeed be individual players with solo potential but, when performing in the orchestra of life, you are best advised to harmonize with the other instruments and the sonics you produce in so doing will make for happiness, contentment, love and *true cosmic harmony amongst yourselves, those with whom you share your planet and the universe in its infinity.* We fully realize that in your present economic climate you are unable to pursue this line of action, as society demands that you work in a factory, office, building site, or whatever, in order to meet your financial commitments. But take heart; after certain events have taken place on your planet in the future, the economy as you know it will no longer exist and, by the time those of you who survive have rebuilt your world, the old ways of doing things will be long-since forgotten and the new order that arises will allow for the accommodation of what we have described above.

Chapter 8

MIKILI

ON THE ARTS AND SCIENCES:

My dear ones, I would like to speak to you on a subject that is often debated vigorously among your intelligentsia: to what extent do the arts and sciences influence (a) your lives as individuals; (b) current trends in sociology, psychology, religion and mysticism; (c) the general evolution of your species on your planet. First of all it is necessary that we effect some distinctions, as the word 'art', for example, covers a broad spectrum of human endeavour.

One of your best selling dictionaries defines the arts as 'the imaginative, creative and non-scientific branches of knowledge considered collectively, especially as studied academically'. However, it is commonly believed by many of you that artistic pursuits are more right-brain than left-brain, while the sciences are viewed conversely. This general picture appears to have arisen from the concept of the stereotyped artist, poet, sculptor, musician or writer, who conducts himself/herself in a bohemian manner and fails to conform to the standards set by society generally. Likewise, the archetypal scientist is a white-coated, bespectacled, introverted personality who seldom mixes outside of his or her own profession. Both these concepts are metaphysically and clinically far from the truth, since social conformity, personal discipline or lack of same, eccentricity and individuation are to be found equally among both the scientific and artistic fraternities, as well as those lay persons who elect to indulge in art or science as hobbies or private interests.

Artists working in the field of commerce are often obliged to keep to strict timetables which necessitate a regimen of discipline in both their private lives and their work, while their freer (if less

110

materially endowed!) colleagues put brush to canvas, pen to paper, hands to keyboard or chisel to stone as and when the spirit moves them. The same applies to those working in the sciences. Long-term research projects that scan several years do not impose the same demands on time and energy as those requiring relatively urgent results.

Many scientists are, in fact, artists, in that they wait for the inspiration to come that will provide that essential break they have been seeking in their research, while there are artists – in the generally accepted meaning of the term – who work purely mechanically and with little right-brain intrusion. Your own Einstein stumbled upon the concept of relativity while dozing on his sickbed; his left brain was in abeyance at the time, thus allowing direct access to the memory-banks of the right-brain. Am I saying that Einstein did not actually *think up* the relativity concept, but rather that he *remembered* it? Yes. All that has ever happened or ever will happen is already on record. All the essence-fragment needs to obtain that information is the correct access code. Now that may sound simple and the question you will naturally ask is, 'Then why can't we all have these codes and find out what we need; surely this would save a lot of suffering in the world?' True. But here is the snag: access codes for each time-band or frequency have to be earned and the learning process via which they are acquired can only be undergone in the hard world of experience or 'university of life', to use one of your own terms. In other words, the more mature the essence-fragment, the more higher-frequency access codes he or she has at his or her disposal; while it should also be borne in mind that there are certain lower frequencies that mankind would do well *not* to access, but more of that shortly. Acquiring the skill to apply these access-codes is, of course, another consideration to be taken into account, because no matter how old the soul or psyche, when it enters a physical body such as your own, it still has to learn from scratch to cope with the mechanisms of that particular brain; although, once these are mastered, its right-brain access will enable it to think years, or even centuries, ahead of its contemporaries.

The arts and the sciences provide expression for both technologists and creative essence-fragments. So no matter how paint-spattered, bohemian in appearance or eccentric your artist, if he or she is simply copying or applying rules already set previously, without originality of any kind, then he or she is as much a technologist as the person with a science degree who simply effects a technological process invented by his or her more creative colleagues. What I am trying to say to you is that original thought, new ideas and discoveries, advanced and more enlightened interpretations of accepted facts, the breaking of virgin ground in any field of endeavour, in fact original or unusual concepts of any kind, are right-brain, whether these come from the worlds of science, the arts, or any other field of human endeavour. Those who set about applying these ideas or discoveries, no matter how advanced their qualifications, are technologists pure and simple, who work more with their left than their right brain hemisphere.

INSPIRATIONAL SOURCES, AND THE EFFECTS OF HALLUCINOGENIC DRUGS:

The facility of right-brain access, however, should not be taken as a guarantee of either the soul-age of the accessor, or the transcendental content of the information or discoveries resulting from that access. The right brain simply acts as a doorway to outer time and those bands or areas in time's circuits that it is able to access will be governed by the maturity or otherwise of the essence-fragment. Certain hallucinatory drugs and chemicals have the effect of loosening the connection between the right and left brain hemispheres; the practice of imbibing these was and still is fashionable in certain sections of your society. But those altered states of consciousness that result from this practice only move the consciousness sideways, for instant evolution or true spiritual revelation cannot be bought with a bottle or tablet; nor is there any drug in existence that can take you beyond that ring-pass-not that is determined by your own stage of spiritual maturity.

In spite of what anyone might tell you to the contrary, hallucinogenic drugs do have a lasting effect on mind, body and psyche, in that they constitute an affront both to the conscious particles of which your body is made and the other members of the group consciousness of which you are an integral part. Such desecration has to be attoned for somewhere along the circuits of time, so do not say you have not been warned.

The employment of hallucinogens to escape from the pressures of your 'real world', or simply as a form of relaxation or entertainment, is one of the symptoms of the malaise from which your species is at present suffering. I know there will be those among you who will not like what I am about to say and will probably blame my channel, but I accept full responsibility when I tell you that truly mature essence-fragments *are born with the awareness of the dangers of hallucinogens – or any chemical dependencies, for that matter – and will avoid them at all costs.* The same also applies to the over-imbibement of alcohol, or any other foodstuff or liquid that interferes with the conscious control of the mind. This is one of the many reasons why old souls are seldom to be found in your `smart sets', or among the self-indulgent rich or materially successful, to whom the participation in certain social rituals is deemed essential to their acceptance among those sections of your society.

QUESTION: Several people I know who were unable to experience an altered state of consciousness naturally were helped to so do by taking drugs. Was this such a bad thing?

ANSWER: And may I make so bold as to ask what happened to these friends of yours, did they truly benefit from their experiences?

QUESTIONER: Well, one of them didn't. He had a nervous breakdown. But he is fine now, although he has to keep away from anything psychic or he becomes ill again. Of the other two, one became very religious and the other latterly took up yoga and now runs classes in yoga and meditation.

ANSWER: Young man, I think you have answered the question for yourself. Your first young friend was shown that the right way for him was to stay firmly planted in the material world, for which experience he came into incarnation in the first place. The other two also found their respective levels, but I can assure you that No.2 would have experienced his 'road to Damascus' quite naturally without the aid of drugs, while the young lady had already felt drawn to the yogic path before she imbibed.

QUESTION: May I ask you, Mikili, what kind of effect drugs, or chemical dependencies, have on the karma of the sufferer and the elements and organisms of which their bodies are composed?

ANSWER: When a person becomes dependent on any form of mind-bending chemical he or she ceases to have control over his or her life. Now is it not logical to assume that, if the natural psyche is not controlling the physical body via the brain, then *something else* *is?* In less serious cases that something may simply be that person's own lower nature, but in most advanced cases the door has been opened to an entity from the lower worlds (of a slower, or lesser evolved frequency than your own) who will delight in amusing itself in an alien body, which it will slowly destroy. Entities of this kind naturally incur bad karma for their destructive acts, but not as severe as the natural essence-fragment who has deliberately reliquished control of its physical vehicle and therefore been the instigator of much suffering.

However, with matters as they are on your planet at the moment, there is an answer to why certain people elect to destroy themselves via the dependency path. As we Paschats and our Crystal cousins have already explained, there are a great many youthful psyches or essence-fragments occupying the body of Gaia, for whom the frequencies are slowly becoming intolerable simply because they are not in harmony with her energies and should not be here in the first place. As Gaia slowly increases the rate of her frequency so more and more of these young souls will seek ways out of the pressure that is building up around them. This will give rise to greater cruelty and aggression, abuse of drugs and foodstuffs generally and an escalation of the final wave of chaos that will precede Gaia's pole shift; but then you have been warned about this by other teachers of light.

Whenever there is an evolutionary quantum leap approaching, those to be affected by it will commence to take sides from quite early on in the proceedings. By 'take sides' I mean their essence-fragments will fall into one of two main categories: (a) those who will be unable to adapt to the new frequency and are therefore destined to abandon their physical bodies and be reborn on a younger planet somewhere else in the universe and (b) those incarnate essence-fragments that are destined to inherit the Earth in the new age or planetary cycle that will follow after the physical manifestations of the quantum leap. This process began on your Earth several years back, but there are still a vast majority of your people who have not yet effected their natural right of choice to jump one way or the other. Many years ago, this was described to our channel in terms of a fissure in the Earth's surface, at first imperceptible, but slowly widening. At first it is so narrow that those in the centre can cross from side to side without difficulty, but as it slowly widens the problems commence and there will eventually come a time when those caught in the middle, who have not effected a choice, will be drawn into the timeless abyss below. In other words, they will become caught in a time-warp from which it will be difficult for them to escape without external assistance.

The last few years in your Earth time have evidenced an escalation in transcendental and inter-cosmic awareness on the one hand and a moral and spiritual degeneration in certain sections of society on the other. This escalation will continue until the differences are far too marked to be ignored worldwide; not that any of you will be able to do much about them; that will be taken care of by Gaia herself, with help from external forces, all of which will be far too powerful to brook any interference from mankind. The Greeks would have referred to this as the wrath of Zeus, the Amerindians would see it as punishment for transgression against the Great Spirit, to the ancient Egyptians it would be Set (chaos) overcoming Osiris (order) and so forth. No doubt your fundamentalists will have a hey-day with quotes from their respective holy books, but may we remind you that the forces of the universe are not swayed by any of the man-made religions popularly favoured by Earth hominids; their concern is for basic cosmic principles and laws. If one of your religions just happens to coincide with those laws, is truly inter-cosmic and respects the equality of and the life-force in *all* things, then the prophecies and workings of that faith will survive the shake-up and flourish thereafter.

ON CHAOS IN ART AND SCIENCE:

At this point I would beg leave of my questionersto return to my original subject matter and consider the effects of both art and science on the earliermentioned categories. Let us start with (a) the effect of the arts and sciences on your lives as individuals, while bearing in mind that both art and science express the principles of order *and* chaos. The kind of art, music, literature or entertainment to which an individual is attracted will serve to highlight the chaos-order ratio within his or her personality, while the same also applies to the world of science. Let us take the latter first, since it will require less elucidation.

Scientists working in fields that are orientated towards the destruction of life and the desecration of Gaia, that disregard the life-force in other species, that contribute towards suffering in both humans and other life-forms on your planet; men and women who will accept any job as long as it pays well regardless of the effects it may have on others, all these are chaos-orientated. Order within the sciences seeks knowledge without causing suffering, respects the planet and those life-forms that dwell thereon and contributes to the well-being of *all*. It is therefore compassionate, caring and gentle, any seemingly harsh decision being effected purely for the good of the whole. What happens in reality, of course, is that most scientists embrace both poles at one time or another during their careers, and it is only when the emphasis falls strongly on one or the other that their preference becomes obvious. The worlds of theoretical physics, quantum mechanics and cosmology have recently spawned a group of scientists who have chosen to acknowledge the metaphysical fields, which signifies a strong swing towards order. The vast majority of what are referred to as scientists, who are really technologists, are content to work in whichever field offers them a fair standard of living, regardless of what this involves esoterically, their respective disciplines having programmed them to disregard anything even bordering on the metaphysical. Unfortunately, it is to the science of the latter that the majority of people look for guidance and, as a consequence, they are misled by the preponderance of chaos within those disciplines. Until the establishments of learning broaden their academic output to embrace the ideas and theories of the more metaphysically inclined among their higher echelons, this sad state will continue.

A balance between chaos and order in either science or art is not a bad thing. Several of your mystical schools teach that the centre path between the two opposing poles is the best road of ascent to the transcendental because it places the traveller in the observation mode, wherein he or she can view both sides *without necessarily becoming caught fast in either.* We have already explained how chaos and order are essential ingredients in the creative recipe and, when it comes to a personal interpretation of these principles, you would do well to bear in mind that *chaos is stimulating to a certain point, beyond which it becomes destructive, while order is relaxing to a certain point, beyond which it veres towards stagnation.*

Now let us turn to the arts. These may be expressed via the purely visual – music, drama, dance, comedy – and any other forms of expression generally classified in the media as entertainment. Without doubt the arts exercise a profound influence on the individual, the media in particular wielding a powerful force in the programming of the individual psyche. We have viewed your media material as shown in many parts of your world and would say without doubt that the accent is more on chaos than order. In fact, we would suggest that there is a glorification of all things chaotic, which has an adverse influence on immature essence-fragments in particular, but also affects those who are on the verge of taking their leave of the fields of cosmic childhood. In case you are not aware of it, your media actually programmes you by dictating the 'norm', or what those in control of the systems feel should be standard behaviour. Therefore, those essence-fragments that are ready to rise to the next stage in their cosmic development feel obliged to stay at the lower frequency for fear of being thought odd or different. It is no use my picking on any particular moral or ethic as I am not of your species anyway, nor have my own people ever been part of an evolutionary stream that is sick.

The glorification of vice, deviations of all kind, violence, cruel competition, the degrading of your females and many, many more attitudes and practices that would not form part of your 'norm', were your species and the planet as a whole on its correct evolutionary path, are symptomatic of the malaise which blinds you to the light of cosmic truth. I would not waste my channel's time outlining the way you would all feel were you cured of your sickness; I fear it would be dismissed as 'boring', 'no fun at all' and 'not natural'. I regret to say that compared with the behaviour of hominids of similar evolutionary status in other parts of the universe it is *you* who are 'unnatural', since you delight in abusing natural *cosmic* laws. So the answer as to whether your media affects you adversely or not must be a positive YES, since the majority of its output is chaos orientated. Before some of you hasten to point out to me that there are programmes that do not exhibit a chaotic content such as those concerned with wildlife, history, geography, the wonders and beauty of your planet, while a good story is always appreciated even by us Paschats and our Crystal cousins, I agree that the occasional spark of cosmic truth does sometimes flash across your screens or broadcasting wavebands. Some of the science fiction to which you are treated, for example, contains more than a grain of truth as you will one day find out to your amazement!

Now let us take a look at what you call music. It is very easy to distinguish the music of chaos from that of order. The former lacks discipline and energizes the lower chakras, while the latter can be either flowing or structured, its emphasis being on the raising of your natural energies from the lower to the higher chakras. In between these two there is a whole range of music that is nondescript as far as the transcendental is concerned. In other words, it does no harm, but neither does it inspire the human spirit to great heights; its value lies purely in its relaxing qualities.

The music favoured by one generation is frequently eschewed by the next, while the former clings with nostalgic tenacity to that with which it was programmed in its youth. The chaotic or orderly quality of any kind of music is easily recognized by the effect it has had on the generation over which it has exerted the most influence. The same applies to rhythms and modes of dance; the controlled but cosmically meaningful movements of the ancient Egyptian temple dancing, for example, constitute a prayer to the light and an acknowledgement of the cosmos, which is more than can be said of some of the gyrations we observe that you have the nerve to classify as 'dancing'. Dancing that lacks discipline, either of rhythm or movement, is by nature chaotic. When a degree of control, no matter how little, enters the picture, the dance begins to assume an order which immediately aligns it with those constant cosmic principles that form part of basic universal understanding. Look to some of your ancient civilizations for clues, Egypt, Greece and India being prime examples. That which flows with the cosmos is orderly; that which goes against the cosmos and its laws is basically chaotic. While both are essential to universal progress, there is such a thing as moderation.

The visual arts are, perhaps, less guilty of chaotic contamination than some of your other forms of creative expression. Chaos in visual art may be evidenced in those more symbolic works which often evoke from the viewer the Philistine remark, 'What is it supposed to be?' Oddly enough, chaos in the visual arts can be stimulating in that it does make people think, or at least try to arrive at some conclusion as to what the artist is actually getting at. Chaos of the human mind, in the form of what you would call madness, or mental derangement, is often evidenced in visual art. Strangely enough it manages to convey a depressive note that is easily perceived by younger essence-fragments who therefore tend to give it a miss, the caption being: 'I'm not having *that* miserable, spooky old thing in *my* living room,' some artist's nightmare being immediately replaced by a set of plastic ducks which look 'much more cheerful'. Our verdict is that more people should take up painting and, incidentally, singing; but we did say *singing* which means using the human voice in the way for which it was constructed, and not as an apology for a screech-machine! But then we Paschats, like most cats, have always had a dislike for a certain kind of noise in particular!

Literature is the next 'art' about which I, or 'we', as I am at present also speaking for Kaini, the Crystal people, and many other beings of pure energy who are genuinely concerned for the welfare of your planet, will proffer our comments. The sad truth is that your literary world, like many other avenues of human endeavour, is controlled by an elite few, who decide for you what you should read and what you should ignore. Under this facade of pseudo-intellectualism there exists a whole body of literature ranging from the obscene to the esoteric that never hits the reviews, but which often provides a more comfortable living for its writers than the former. What most people read is usually dictated by the advertisers; a few strange posters dotted here and there will often arouse the curiosity of those who would not normally think of browsing round a bookshop, whereas dedicated seekers after truth will spare no effort or expense in their quest for written answers to what they view as life's enigmas. Strangely enough we do not consider all 'elite' literature as orderly and unacknowledged efforts as chaotic. Indeed, the reverse can often be the case, but then we are more concerned with content than literary merit. So, if the content of a written work stimulates the reader's desire for cosmic knowledge and the pursuit of the virtues of caring, love, gentleness and understanding, then we would view that author's offering as being a representation of the path of order. But if that literature, no matter how erudite its literary content, conspires to lure the reader onto the path of hedonism, selfishness, physical and mental violence and the abuse of any other life form, then its author is truly an emissary of the lords of chaos!' Knowledge of chaos and the destruction it leaves in its wake is, however, essential to your education. It is only when you start to bring it into your own lives, to the extent that others suffer as a result, that it becomes an abomination.

Referring to (b) and (c) as mentioned above, the influence of both the arts and sciences on sociology, psychology, religion and mysticism must by now be abundantly clear. As to the general evolution of your planet, until the energies of both aspects are evenly balanced, your world will continue to suffer, albeit unnecessarily. We hear you talk of 'people power' that topples governments, changes established regimes overnight and alters world economy. Were you to have applied even a little of that power to your development as separate and discrete *cosmic* beings or, as some of you might prefer to put it, 'concentrate more on your spiritual (as against religious!) development', you could have saved your world from the forthcoming disaster. But it is now too late, as we who exist in timelessness foresaw that it would be, so we can but stand by and hope that our few words of advice might point those who survive the cataclysm in a more orderly cosmic direction.

QUESTION: Surely you are being presumptuous in trying to foist your morals and ethics on us. Since you are not of our planet, or even our species, how do you know how we feel or what we need?

ANSWER: How do *you* know what the other species with whom you share your planet feel and need? It is obvious that you do not or you would allow them the freedom you so crave for yourselves. Does a cow actually *wish* to be brutally killed and its flesh eaten? Does a fox or a badger actually *wish* to be tom to pieces for your amusement? Do your trees enjoy having their life cycles ended abruptly to suit your economic needs? Do your laboratory animals enjoy being used in painful and needless experiments? Do your sea-creatures enjoy swimming in polluted waters? And how many of your own womenfolk really like being treated as slaves or second class citizens? We could go on and on. You have not learned to accord to the other species with which you share the planet those courtesies upon which you yourselves place so much importance. You demand freedom and a certain standard of living, *at the expense of others, even of your own kind!*

We know exactly what you feel because we are able to penetrate your minds. And we know what you *would feel* were you not afflicted by the cosmic illness from which many of you suffer. Rest assured that the second option would make you infinitely happier than the first. You should know from your own experience that, when either you or one of your number is sick, in pain, or afflicted by a high temperature, your reasoning powers run amok and you do not view life in quite the same way as you do when you are feeling fit. Transposing this to a cosmic level might help you to understand what we are trying to say to you. Believe us when we tell you that after the next quantum leap, with its accompanying telluric phenomena, mankind's ethics and morals will alter drastically. In fact, were you to be confronted by your greatgreat grandchildren at this very moment, we regret to inform you that they would castigate you in much stronger terms than we would dream of employing; but we are content to let time do its work. The resentment you hold in your heart against us and what we have said cannot in any way hurt us; it can only rebound on you. And please do not seek a scapegoat in our channel, as she is none too happy about the firmness of our admonitions on certain points. Not that she does not agree with us, but she fears that our words might be a little too strong. We think not, however, and rest on our judgement.

QUESTION: As an artist I do not feel I want to conform to society, so you might think I am what you term 'bohemian'. But I try not to hurt anyone, I follow the Green Party and I spend my free time helping animals. However, I am not very disciplined in that I do not keep office hours and I work when I feel inspired. Does that make me an agent of chaos?

ANSWER: Good gracious, no. It is possible to go over the top on personal discipline. In fact, it can become an illness in some people. There is a subtle difference in doing your own thing if it only affects you and pleasing yourself at the expense of others. For example, if you choose (as we observe that you do) to rise from your bed at midday and work into the early hours of the following morning, as long as you are alone and have only yourself to please, then that is between you and your body. But should your unusual hours deny food or sleep to a child that had to attend school the following day, cause problems for a partner who was obliged to observe more generally accepted working hours, then the element of selfishness creeps in and the suffering caused thereby is the first step in the erection of a karmic edifice that has to be demolished in some way or other along the avenues of time.

Where personal discipline is concerned, excesses in either direction can lead to psychic fragmentation. The unbendable disciplinarian who is unable to accept that circumstances arise in life wherein there has to be some giving will, like the proverbial reed in your holy book that 'bends not in the wind', surely break!

This is precisely why certain psychological types are more prone to nervous breakdowns than others. In times of extreme stress you need the strength of character to keep going, but at the same time *adapt* to the situation, whatever it might be. In other words, a combination of mental discipline, sensitivity, adaptability and resilience is the best mental medicine to see you through.

QUESTION: I work in the sciences, but please do not mention my name in your book or I might lose my job! On the level at which I work, however, one does not get much chance to be creative. The really creative work goes to those on research grants, which means they have probably qualified at one of the major universities. What you might be interested to know, however, is that both myself and the majority of my colleagues are with you on the Gaian side. Our very work demonstrates to us the oneness of life, so how can we deny it? Of course, there are some among us who consider their fellow workers as cranks or 'nutters', but we have a rude word to describe them which I would not dare to repeat to you. What I would like to ask you, on my own behalf and that of my colleagues at work is, will there be a time in the future when the kind of orthodox scientific establishment for which we work will openly embrace the metaphysical world? Or are we pipe-dreaming?

ANSWER: No, you are not over-indulging your imagination. That time will come and the circumstances surrounding it will be as astounding and unexpected as the sudden, radical changes in the world arena have been to many a diehard, diplomat in the early nineteen-nineties. It will only take one small and seemingly insignificant episode to turn the tables. But more I cannot tell you, as those who are destined to effect these happenings are already in position. I think you call them 'sleepers' in your spy stories, no?

QUESTION: I and my friends have read several books purporting to be teachings from extraterrestrial intelligences, some of which claim to belong to intergalactic 'organizations' with grand titles. How can ordinary people like ourselves, who are not psychic, but anxious to learn about the universe, tell who is or is not deceiving us?

ANSWER: There are several pointers by which you can recognize the authenticity (or otherwise) of an extraterrestrial agent of the light. Here are a few to start with: note the attitude adopted towards the individual, whether it be one of your kind, our kind, an animal, a plant etc. If it is one of openheartedness, love, caring and understanding, then you are dealing with an entity of light. Should the message on the other hand involve an impersonal approach, intolerance of the feelings and expressions of others, exclusivity, you know the kind of thing – 'we, and we only, know it all, are the greatest, brook no argument or discussion, are not interested in anyone else's approach no matter how genuine, you do it our way or else' – and so forth, rest assured that neither we Paschats, the Crystal people, or our special Lizard and Dolphin friends are behind it. However, it is not our place to pass judgement, since there are those who do not necessarily respond to our particular approach. But, being the tender-hearted creatures that we are, for us the love principle is the most important thing in the universe. And as to the authenticity of much of what is purported to come from extraterrestrial (or supramundane) sources, regrettably it does not!

Chapter 9

THE CRYSTAL PEOPLE

COSMIC CREATIVITY AND ITS DIVERSE MANIFESTATIONS:

In *THE LION PEOPLE,* our Paschat cousins have previously explained how their species and ours evolved from a specific cosmic impulse, which produced the evolutionary strain that was to manifest ultimately as the leonids and hominids that we became. Our genetic codes were therefore formulated from that primary impulse and we feel we would like to expound on this theme.

What we are basically dealing with here is the subject of creativity, which follows on naturally from information given in earlier communications (see Chapter 3) on the one hand and the age-old arcane teaching in your own mystery schools that you are all `gods in the making' on the other.

Just as you utilize the materials available to you in the natural course of your lives, shaping them as you wish to create the amenities of what you term 'civilization', so do essence-fragments existing within faster wave-bands make use of the energies available to them to produce creations appropriate to their position on the evolutionary scale. The only difference lies in the fact that, whereas very few of you are aware of the consciousness and life-force that pulsates through all of those things of which you make convenient use, essence-fragments that have cosmically individuated (become one with their antiparticles, thus creating the energy thrust necessary to take them to the next dimension) do acknowledge the individuality of that life-force, and make a point of consulting with it first before utilizing it for creative purposes which automatically subject it to a given set of experiences.

Some of you will, no doubt, catch our mention of an 'energy thrust from one dimension to another' so we had better explain: the gamma ray emitted when a particle joins with its antiparticle also has another, more subtle aspect that has so far escaped your technological observations, but which your theoretical physicists will become aware of in the not-too-distant future. Whereas the gamma ray (being part of the spectrum of your world and therefore recordable on your instrumentation) remains in the particle-wave packet's old orbit, i.e. matter, its higher frequency energy emission propels that new consciousness that emerges from the coupling into the next dimension wherein it once again forms into another 'particle-wave packet'. This process is, in fact, infinite. So the 'now you see it, now you don't' annihilation believed to result from the particle-antiparticle coupling is a misunderstanding based on insufficient technical data concerning life in other dimensions or parallel universes. As we explained earlier, what really happens is that the conjoined pair leave your material universe and enter a more subtle dimension wherein they *are no longer observable* from your universe, since they do not resonate at your physical frequency.

Now let us take a look at your own efforts at creation. These take many forms, from the literature and arts Mikili has already discussed with you to the construction of matter in the form of buildings, technology and agriculture; in fact, the manipulation of all things material. As we have already discussed, all of these manifestations of frozen energy only appear as physical and solid to you because you observe them as such. Were you to exist on a higher frequency, you would be able to look at a table and note that instead of viewing a solid object you would see a collection of particles, atoms, molecules or whatever, loosely connected to *give the effect* of solidity. And, of course, were you to be undergoing your experience in a universe parallel to the one you observe at present, particularly if that world moved at a frequency that was even fractionally faster than your 'here and now', you would be able to pass easily through your table, door, wall and other earthly 'haunts', just as your wave aspect does while its particle, your body, is sound asleep!

Our next consideration is the pros and cons of effecting the creative process without the prior consent of the consciousness involved. A hypothetical example might help, so let us say that one of your architects designs a house for a building firm. His designs are harmonious in that they blend well with the environment and contain excellent home potential. The creative process has begun. The designs being acceptable to the builders and the quantity surveys agreed, suitable materials are purchased and the foundations are laid. However, there are three major issues at stake here: the proposed site, the nature of the materials to be employed in the project and the attitudes of those engaged in the erection of the structure. Let us take the site first. Your Chinese geomancers would apply their *feng shui* to define whether the location was conducive to a private residence and, if so, which way should it face? In other words, they would consult the Earth itself to see if the placing of a building at that spot was acceptable to Gaia. Our hypothetical builder, however, has no such exalted principles, since he has not the slightest idea that the ground upon which he proposes to construct his edifice of bricks and mortar has a consciousness and might therefore like to have even a small say as to what is parked on its surface! Now to point two. Building materials these days are often mass-manufactured, the constituents being thrown together for convenience and speed without forethought as to whether or not they blend harmoniously, which in many cases they do not.

Now man enters the picture, as it is mostly the males of your species to whom the job of laying foundations and placing brick upon brick usually falls. For the sake of argument let us take two examples here, the first representing a harmonious set-up, the ground at that spot being quite happy about having a residence placed upon it, the materials employed having no problems in their relationship with each other and the workmen involved, being of benign disposition, apply themselves cheerfully to their task. The result when finished will therefore be a happy residence that will welcome its future inhabitants with open arms; or, to put it another way, the outcome of this creative venture will be a lucky dwelling, conducive to harmonious family relations. Few of you are aware of the powerful influence your habitat can have upon your psychology.

Now let us assume a different stance and suppose the ground upon which the dwelling is to be built objects to its use for this particular purpose. Perhaps it would rather be a leafy wood or an open field or maybe, if it has to accept a building, it would prefer a school of laughing children or a hospital where its healing energies could be put to good use. Therefore, when the builders arrive to lay the foundations, there is something of a resentment, while the building materials are shoddy and lacking in harmony one with another. To add to this chaotic collection, the workmen employed have no interest in their jobs other than as a means of livelihood and could not care less how the house turns out as long as they are adequately compensated for their 'between tea-breaks' labour. When that house, that creation, is completed, whoever moves into it will be sure to encounter difficulties, frustrations and disharmonies in their own life. Creations effected without the prior consent and cooperation of the materials concerned will not, by their very nature, emit harmonious energies.

In days gone past on your planet more care was taken to observe these small courtesies, just as your craftpersons took pride in their work. This resulted in happy dwellings and beautiful creations which have endured as heritage houses and antiques. Do you see what we are getting at? But because your planet is grossly overcrowded, in order to provide shelter for your numerous peoples, you are obliged to molest its natural energies to the point of causing them distress, which is then passed on to the unfortunate tenants who are of your own kind. Such are the problems caused when the creators are insensitive to their materials. Perhaps we could liken it to a child let loose in a laboratory, the odds against his creating an explosion rather than a beneficial blending being high, to say the least.

One of the first things your species will have to come to terms with when it takes its next step up the evolutionary ladder will be an acknowledgement of and communication with all other life-forces or consciousness. Although we have said this already, we cannot emphasize it enough. Then and then only will you commence to be truly gods in the making, as to be a 'god' in the esoteric meaning of the word implies a cognizance of the virtues of love, understanding and caring, all of which are prerequisite to the *harmonious* creative process. Ah, you will say, but are there not evil gods who erect evil edifices and create evil species? There are certainly beings who are out of their correct time sequence, for example yourselves and others in the universe like you. Such beings draw their creative energies from others rather than from the wisdom, knowledge and light of the universe itself and, in order to obtain these energies, they subject their charges to a kind of spiritual slavery. They blind them to the light of cosmic truth with false religious and sociological dogmas and doctrines and proceed to feed upon the energies engendered by the suffering of their charges, just as the building materials and the patch of Earth mentioned in the example given above suffered because they were not *free,* or acknowledged as having the right to think and decide for themselves. The majority of your people are, we regret to say, subject to this slavery.

We must be fair, however, and say that not all of you are effecting the creative process with deliberate intent to enslave. Insensitivity to the life-force in all things can also result from the pure ignorance of spiritual immaturity. In other words, you yourselves have not been programmed to this knowledge and, being cosmically immature, you have not attained the degree of awareness necessary to comprehend and logicize it. You therefore proceed about your creative processes in blissful ignorance of the harm, or good for that matter, that you might be doing to other intelligences and your karmic patterns develop accordingly. Your attitude towards your own bodies is a typical example of this, many of you failing to realize that the organisms that rely on your soma for their existence constitute a whole eco-system. When this system is functioning in balance you enjoy good health, but when that order turns to chaos you find yourself faced with dis-ease; and yet, rather than change your ways, you continue to effect the abuse that has caused that imbalance, thus expediting your demise. If you were to be aware of and in touch with, or sensitive to the needs of that group consciousness that is your personal eco-system, you would save yourself, and it, a lot of unnecessary suffering.

You have a saying 'ignorance of the law is no excuse'; the same applies exactly in the cosmic scheme of things. As children you may desecrate a work of art, wilfully destroy those toys that some creative person has painstakingly assembled, cause pain to those who love you and abuse help afforded to you. But as you mature you should become aware of these finer points and adjust your thoughts and actions accordingly. If you do not, then the wheel of karma as you call it will revolve, with you in one of its spokes, until you do. And, incidentally, cosmic (or karmic) laws know no physical age group. Problems arising between parents and children, teachers and their charges, or older pupils and their tutors, all have to be worked through eventually, if not in this time-zone or universe, then in another. So by disciplining your young and enlightening them on these matters from an early age you are, in fact, doing them a favour, *as long as you are not forcing them into something for which they are not yet ready.* In other words, pass on the information and then it is up to each individual essence-fragment to use it as he or she may according to his or her stage of spiritual maturity.

ARCHONIC EVOLUTION:

Let us now consider the creative process from a cosmological standpoint as carried out in the correct way, that being in accordance with the forward-directional impulses of cosmic law. All cosmic events, in all universes, including your own, are orchestrated by intelligences to whom this task falls according to the natural order of things. Your metaphysicians have given these various names according to the specific mystery school involved, devas, archangels, archons, daemons and so forth. Who are these intelligences, you may ask? Are they essence-fragments from the hominid genus or were they born and nurtured in some other universe which houses life-forms such as you would never dream of? Since it is neither of these let us explain to you who they are and whence they come. They come from all over the universe, having originated among what your ancients would refer to as `the primary four', but which you would probably know as the spirits of fire, air, water and earth. These essence-fragments commence their evolutionary cycles as single particles, each of which is associated primarily with a specific function. Fire, for example, fuses and refines, air conveys information and disperses the seeds and spores which water fructifies and endows with the quality of feeling, while the solidifying energies of earth provide the foundation which acts as a springboard towards further evolutionary progress.

As each single element evolves it conjoins with a different element, thereby becoming a duality; air-fire, for example, or water-earth. This is followed in turn by a threefold relationship and finally, when the fourfold nature is attained, a merging with the antiparticle is achieved and that fourfold consciousness assumes its place among the deva or archonic kingdoms. It is then involved in an entirely new creative process in that whereas it had formerly been under the direction of senior devic intelligences, it will now have a territory of its own consisting of elements as yet single, twofold or threefold, with which to effect its own creative patterns while it, in turn, will come under the jurisdiction of those more powerful archonic intelligences that formulate the blueprints for whole universes. So the process continues through each finer and faster frequency until a point is reached at which all creation blends. At that point all time is one, so all that has ever happened in the infinity of all universes, throughout all times, through the various sequences of chaos and order, is known, experienced and fully understood *instantaneously*. *Thus,* every feeling, thought, action and expression of the 'self,' no matter what form that self may take, be it hominid, leonid, reptilian, elemental, or any other of the divers manifestations of creation throughout infinity, is adding to or, since we are dealing with timelessness, *has added* to the whole. That whole is what you would call God, although there is no single god as such, but simply a state of creativity that accommodates all 'gods in the making', including *all other life forms* which, like yourselves, are sparks of a grand divine creative fire. The Paschats referred to this creative state as 'the Old Ones', to us in our physical world it was 'the Infinite Prism', to the Lizard people of Auriga it is 'the Breathers of Fire'; each species has its own name for divinity. And, by way of reinforcing what the Paschats have already told you, there is no 'hot-line' to this ultimate state, the only way to return to the creator is along the rocky and danger-strewn path of personal evolution. Between what you are now and the end of your journey any prayers addressed direct to this creative beingness or deity are dealt with according to the particular level of the supplicant, sometimes by his or her transpersonal self (divine spark) and at others by caring intermediaries. To use once more one of your own terms of expression: God delegates!

THE HOMINID ROLE IN THE ARCHONIC CREATIVE PROCESS:

Having identified the archonic kingdoms let us now show you where you, as hominids, fit into the universal, creative picture, once you have individuated beyond the need for experience in the fields of dense matter. There is obviously a point at which a mature hominid essence-fragment, or a Paschat come to that, participates with the archonic kingdoms in the creative process and this is how it takes place: the early structures of a physical universe are orchestrated by the archons, as we have already explained. These same beings, working with the primary four, bring a planet to a state where it is ready to receive different life-forms, one of which will eventually become the dominant species thereon. Let us take your own planet as an example. After it had settled down and was ready to accept what you would view as the first life-forms, mature essence-fragments from each of the new lifeforms entered the picture and cast their creative influences over the infant essence-fragments of their own kind that were ready to undergo the ensoulment process. This was achieved with harmony and precision. No problems. As has already been explained to you, the initial species that was to create an environment for the hominids, who were destined by design to become the dominant species on your particular world, came up against difficulties which stunted their evolution and obliged the more evolved essence-fragments among them to withdraw. The reason for this has already been clarified. So at what point did the hominid influence enter? It first cast its energies onto your planet while the Lizard people were endeavouring to prepare the ground for the eventual descent of its (hominid) kind into matter.

Let us explain how this process works. In your case there was not one but five highly evolved hominid essence-fragments to whom the task of planting the correct evolutionary seed fell. But unfortunately their preparatory work coincided with the arrival of the cosmic virus, about which we and the Paschats have already told you. Now each of the five beings of light concerned represented specific energies that were deemed essential to the healthy growth and development of Homo sapiens. These were as follows:

(1) Stability; (2) fertility; (3) equilibrium (balance);
(4) love/understanding; and (5) inter-cosmic awareness.

Each of these principles also resounded at many octaves. Stability, for example, represented the security and binding force that allows for the expansion of growth; fertility was concerned not only with human reproduction but also with agriculture, forestry, genetics etc. and the development of the arts, beauty, natural pleasure and appreciation of the manifestation of the infinite within the finite; equilibrium referred to the divine balance between chaos and order and, at the human level, the natural equality of and mutual respect for all sexes and species within the spectrum of that creation; love/understanding carried shamanic overtones in that it embraced an understanding and love of all things; and inter-cosmic awareness designated the essencefragment's awareness of its place in the cosmic scheme of things, at any one time, and its true cosmic roots. Unfortunately, due to the influence of the virus, Earth hominids chose to abuse their five principles, with particular accent on numbers 2 and 3, thus rejecting their true rulers of light and electing to follow the path of chaos. By acting thus, they attracted unto themselves, as their ruling influence, a chaotic entity of a power-seeking order that feeds upon strife and suffering; and your mythical 'fall from Eden' had begun. So, you see, your Satanic forces are of your own creation. They feed on your negative energies and the only way this chaotic influence can be removed is by the frequency on your planet being raised to a level that it and those among you who feed it cannot tolerate.

For your information, the ancient Egyptians named these five influences Osiris, Horns, Set, Isis and Nephthys and ascribed to them the five extra days acquired in your calendar as a result of the last evolutionary quantum leap that involved a pole shift. The story of the overthrow of Osiris (order) by Set (chaos) and the flight of Isis to the wilderness is basically the ancient Egyptian story of the fall of your planet. The original influence of Set was not, in fact, an evil one, but simply represented the order/chaos balance (polarity) that applies throughout the universe. But, in rejecting the order aspect of that balance and favouring the power-seeking dominance of chaos, mankind rejected the natural cosmic order of things, thereby placing itself outside the protection of that hominid being of light who could have helped you to make your planet a much, much happier place; one in which the suffering on a grand scale, that you have been subjected to over the aeons and will be also in the not too distant future, could have been avoided. On the other hand, as has been pointed out by some of your esotericists, the disharmony prevalent on your Earth has provided a honing process for those evolving essence-fragments that have seen fit to make use of as a springboard in their ascent to the faster frequencies.

Of course, the above names should not be taken as 'gospel', since they are only one nation's interpretation of the personal sonics of the essences concerned. In the pre-Egyptian and Sumerian civilizations of Atlantis and Mu those essences were known by other names, while your various religions have added their nomenclatures to the list over the ages. This inevitably raises the question as to who is the rightful ruling essence, or deva as you prefer to call them, of your planet and of your Moon, for that matter. In order to explain this we will need to have recourse to your mythology, for therein lie the clues.

The ancient Egyptians, who culled their knowledge from the Atlantean colonists who settled on their shores prior to the last pole shift experienced on your planet, gave a specific order for the 'birth' of the five epagomenal gods or neters, while their own tradition also insists that these neters were not all born on the same 'day'. Osiris was born on the first day, Horns on the second, Set on the third, Isis on the fourth and Nephthys on the fifth. The first, third and fifth of these epagomenal days were considered unlucky, but the fourth is described in the ancient texts as 'a beautiful festival of heaven and earth'.[1] The term 'days' actually refers to long periods of time, during which each of these essences endeavoured to exert their individual energies on the creative processes. If it is of any help to you to know, you are actually in the third stage at the moment; the other two stages, which will emphasize the feminine, yin or anima among your kind, are still to come.

QUESTION: Some of your listeners and, no doubt, many of your readers will be interested in and perhaps working in the fields of healing. Could you tell us which of the five essences of light you have mentioned represents healing, in all its manifestations?

ANSWER: We fear you might not like this answer, but in truth it is number three, since balance or equilibrium is an essential prerequisite to good physical and mental health. However, all five do emit energies that can aid that balance so, if you have an invocation or prayer in mind, you would be advised to address it to all of them; and, since the third manifestation has been temporarily deposed, you will need to draw to a certain extent on your own inner spiritual resources to compensate for the imbalances brought about by your fellow men and women.

QUESTION: Could you please explain how these five essences or deities came to be associated with the five extra days, and why are they referred to among ancient records as actual people rather than devas or planetary rulers?

ANSWER: To answer the last part of your question first, because they were of hominid and not of devic origin. Secondly, the old Atlantean priesthood were familiar with the original plan and, although they passed this information to the indigenous populations of the lands they colonized, it eventually became either encoded

---

1 *The Gods of the Egyptians.* E.A. Wallis Budge, vol. 2, p. 109.

in myth, or degenerated into religious superstition. Since the five epagomenal days were visited upon the Earth following the arrival, on Egyptian and other shores around the Atlantic seaboard, of these priestly rulers, it was only natural that the additional days should become associated with the names and titles of these tall, handsome newcomers, who displayed a knowledge of science (seen as magic by the lesser lettered) far beyond that of their host nations. The passage of time saw these nomenclatures translated into the various native tongues and eventually absorbed into the local deities of the lands concerned. It should also be borne in mind that the Atlantean settlers did not all arrive at one time. Earlier colonists in Egypt, for example, appeared on those shores many, many years before the Atlantic continent was destroyed. However, since myth is more often than not a physical enaction of a divine plan, the story of Isis, Osiris and their family. may be read at any of several levels.

QUESTION: Does each of the major deities have different aspects, which could be related to his or her chakras and which manifest in much the same way that certain energy-levels in our own bodies are triggered off when the respective chakras are activated? For example, I am a devotee of the goddess Isis and it strikes me that other goddesses, Aphrodite for example, could be simply expressions of the one being from her different chakras?

ANSWER: This is quite true, in fact, since the goddess energies of which you speak are limited in quality to the stage of development of the recipients at any given time in their personal cycles of cosmic maturation, or the overall evolutionary pattern of the group entity or manifest level of consciousness through which they are experiencing. This naturally begs for the question, 'Do the deities, then, have chakras?' What you refer to as chakras are merely points of contact between the essence-fragment and its divine source. But since the frequency gap between each fragment and the total essence varies according to its stage of maturity, chakras may be viewed as connecting points between the manifest fragment and the next waveband into which it will eventually move in its ascent to the finer frequencies or, in the terms of your own esotericists, the link between the physical and etheric bodies.

QUESTION: You haven't yet told us the names of the hominid beings of light who are the rightful rulers of the Earth and the Moon, or are you deliberately avoiding that one?

ANSWER: Not at all. Very soon the chains of chaos will be broken and Gaia and all her children will be finally freed of its fetters. The new ruling influence on your planet will then be predominantly feminine or yin, while your Moon will assume its true polarity, which is masculine, or yang. We expect you want names, as Earth hominids do so like to pigeonhole everything! Well, you may give your new ruling lady what names you wish: Isis, Demeter, Gaia, Danuih (her old Atlantean name); and her lunar consort: Michael, Anubis, Merlin, Akhantuih (also Atlantean). It matters not as long as the basic energies – *and polarity emphasis* – of the essences are acknowledged and respected. If you are among those who can only conceive of lunar energies in female terms we suggest you consult some of your earlier myths, notably the Egyptian, where your night luminary is accorded its correct polarity as Thoth or Tehuti, whose association with time, and the acquisition of the five epagomenal days, should afford you some clues as to the nature of this deity, his country of origin, and the stellar influence he carries.

QUESTION: Am I right in assuming that these hominid beings of light who were concerned with the growth and development of Earth people were of Crystal hominid origin, which is why your peoples, and the Siriun energies, are so bound up with this planet?

ANSWER: You are quite correct. Those five aforementioned hominid-type essences who were designated by the infinite prism as responsible for the development and spiritual growth of the hominid strain on your planet were originally Crystal people, although they commenced their evolutionary cycle in a galaxy that was to the Siriun system what Sirius is to your Sun and her solar family. This is why certain factions among your students of the esoteric are inclined to point the finger of blame for the fall at Sirius. But do bear in mind that it was *your* ancestors (and many of you to this day) who rejected our energies of light and opted for the more tempting path of chaos.

We anticipate the question: 'Can you tell us which star (in the universe that is visible to us) you came from before you went to the Siriun system?' Sorry, but we are not prepared to give you a name at this moment in your time, as that discovery constitutes part of your own learning and development. But since there is no such thing as coincidence, if you consult your star charts you might, by chance, stumble upon the right 'neck of the universal woods', so to speak.

135

QUESTION: So now we have established your role in our destiny, how and where do the leonine essences fit in with all this, and why are they concerned with the welfare of our planet?

ANSWER: Aside from the Siriun connection, leonine or feline essences generally play a very distinct role in the cosmic scheme of things which you may not be aware of. The 'old ones' allotted jointly to them and a certain fiery devic order the task of maintaining universal parity between chaos and order so that, wherever either axis of this polarity becomes over-accentuated, it falls to these essences to redress the balance and restore equilibrium. You will find all the clues you need in your mythology, especially the Egyptian. Some of your metaphysicians and mystics have been known to refer to an order of cosmic beings whom they have designated as 'the occult police' which, bearing in mind the attitude of many of you on your planet towards your own police forces, is hardly flattering. However, this 'force' which consists mainly of fiery devic (Seraphim in your angelic terminology) and leonid essences is a reality, although it bears no relationship to any organization similarly named on your planet. Of that we *do* assure you.

Chapter 10

SUMMARY, EVIDENCE AND COMMENTS

As the channeller for these texts I must confess to experiencing difficulty in justifying much of the information contained therein, my communicators having presented me with certain scientific-type data that cannot, for the present anyway, be substantiated; while also making statements concerning the history of this planet and the Atlantean episode in particular, some of which do not accord with standard western metaphysical beliefs. However, I am duty bound to present what I am given and, were I to 'doctor' it to fit in with those popularly espoused traditions, I would not be able to live with myself. There is one point that needs to be made quite clear at this juncture: *I make no claim whatsoever to having the final word on the subject matter raised therein, nor, as a channeller, do I lay title to absolute accuracy. As* essence-fragments incarnate in hominid bodies on a 'fallen planet' none of us can be absolutely sure that we, and we only, are divinely inspired, any such pretence naturally demanding a psychological assessment of 'delusions of grandeur'. I can only put on paper that which I am 'given', within the limitations of my own 'self', in the spirit of honesty and truth and with a sincere and selfless desire to serve the essences of light and love that strive to make this planet a better place for all concerned. Having said my piece let me now attend to the task of rationalizing some of the information given in the light of knowledge ancient and modern.

Until recently the images of beings with the upright stance of a hominid, but with the head and features of a leonid were confined to various early mythologies, notably the Egyptian, wherein goddesses such as Sekhmet and Tefnut and the god Mihos (Maahes), son of the cat goddess Bast, made their appearances along with other animal-headed deities; and the ancient Hindu texts in which the

137

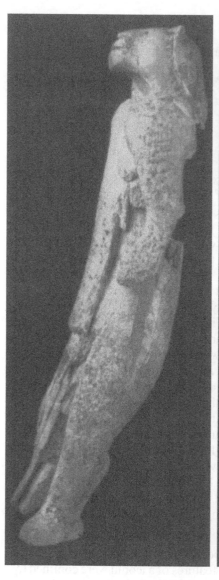 

lion man, or 'tawny one', was believed to be the 4th incarnation of the god Vishnu. Orthodox scholars take pre-dynastic Egypt back to the 4th to 5th millennium BC, but no earlier and, although more specialized researchers in these fields have suggested a considerably greater antiquity, such theories are still viewed as questionable by many of the recognized institutes of learning.

A fairly recent discovery at Hohlenstein-Stadel (Baden Wurtenburg, Germany), however, plays havoc with the more conservatively inclined schools of anthropology and archaeology, since it features an ivory statuette with a leonine head on a human body which can be dated back to around 32,000BC. The excavation was executed under the direction of Elisabeth Schmid and the findings later confirmed by Joachim Hahn, H. Muller-Beck, W. Taute and R. Wetzel. Here is the description given by the above mentioned authorities, as presented by the Ulmer Museum, Ulm, Germany:

'The statuette presents a human body, on which an animal's head is placed. This head, with the ears directed to the front, is of a feline animal, in concentrated attention, clear to attack. The mane are absent and so one can think of a lioness' head. In proportion to the head the body is too long. On the place of the chest and the abdomen a part has come loose and is lost. The most interesting part of the right hand side of the body and the right arm could not directly be fitted to the body. The left arm hangs along the body; in the upper part were made seven carvings. On the legs the original surface is, partly undamaged, conserved. The back of the knee, muscles of the calf and the feet were worked with care. The sole of the feet lays in a small angle with respect to the length axis of the statue and suggests that the artwork could not stand erect without support.

'Even if the statue was found in so many pieces, yet it is possible, following recent studies, to conclude that the maker did not want to make the image of a man but of a woman with a lion's head. On the belly, below the navel, one discovers a horizontal carving, which corresponds with the folds of the abdomen, characteristic for female figures. The triangular zone on the lower part of the torso also reminds us of the female sex. The smooth, sloping plane beneath the throat, portrays a separation of the breasts. One has also a fragment, which could not be fitted directly to the statue, which is more than probable a piece of the breasts.'

Certain grammatical inconsistencies in the above are, no doubt, due to the translation from the original German to English, but the description is, nevertheless, more than adequate.

A further note from the Museum describes Hohlenstein as:

'... a rocky elevation on the south slopes of the valley of the river Lone in the Zwabische Jura, north of the Ulm-Danube. In this elevation are two caves, The Barenhohle (bears cave) and the cave of Stadel, which is 50m deep...The stratigraphy of the site consisted of a 5.50m thick packet in which several archaeologic layers were following each other, mainly belonging to the Middle-Palaeolithic, the Aurignacian – and the Magdalene – period.'

One particular phrase in the above comments caught my eye and that was the reference to the body being too long in proportion to the head. If any of my readers keep cats, I would suggest that they take note of the ratio of the head to the body when their pets stand on their hind legs. Look, also, at the formation of the leg structure when the feline is in the erect position and I think you will see that the statuette figured above does not relate to a hominid woman shaman, as would be popularly supposed, but to an all-feline being *who has learned to stand and function in the upright position, just as we do.* Think about it!

It would certainly appear that Paschats were 'in evidence' long before the rise of Egypt, or archaic India for that matter, although, no doubt, the tradition carried right through to those ancient peoples from some long-forgotten star-culture about which we have little information and even less empirical evidence.

Latest fossil-dating techniques are also playing havoc with generally accepted evolutionary theories. The fossilized skeleton of a boy found in a cave near Nazareth, for example, is 100,000 years old, which means that modern humans cannot be descended from Neanderthal man! Should any of my readers wish to substantiate this for themselves, this find and others complementary to it were featured in the Channel 4 television programme *Equinox* on 10th November, 1991.

THE AGE OF THE SPHINX?

My contacts have always urged me to forgo discussions and debates concerning the information they give me as, sooner or later, it will be ratified by the scientific establishment. One such revelation, that appeared in *The Daily Mail,* 4 October, 1991, confirmed the suggestion I made in my *book Ancient Egypt: The Sirius Connection* that the Sphinx was not constructed by the Pharaoh Kephren as was generally believed, but that he had the face of the earlier structure, which was originally all-lion, altered to that of his own visage. The report read as follows:

> 'The Great Sphinx of Egypt is much older than was thought claim geologists. Researchers using seismic testing at the site for the first time conclude that an ancient civilization, carved the sphinx between 5000 and 7000 BC - at least 2,500 to 4,500 years earlier than has been accepted... Its creation is traditionally attributed to the Pharaoh Khafre. The new study, led by Boston University geologist Robert M. Schoch, suggests that Khafre merely restored the monument.'Testing by sound waves to establish depths of corrosion of subsurface limestone rock structures indicates that the front and sides of the Sphinx were not carved at the same time as its rear.'

As I have previously suggested, it was originally *all lion.*

The Crystal people tell us that they originated in a hominid strain not dissimilar to our own, so for many they will be easier to come to terms with than the Paschats. Having 'worked' with the two races, however, both in the 'now' and in my former leonid lives, I can make one suggestion which is based on the basic nature of each species: the Crystal people are essentially cerebral, and inclined to be clinical and to the point, which could be interpreted by some water-orientated (emotionally motivated) Earth hominids as cold and unfeeling, while others among us might appreciate their propensity for 'calling a spade a spade'. The Paschats, on the other hand, are warm, earthy beings, who contrast generously with their Crystal cousins. Thus the two races, in true Siriun fashion, form a complement, one to the other.

One of the questions I am often asked when lecturing on subjects bordering on the extra-terrestrial is:

'Do you have any proof that the hominid form is not the most evolved in the universe, because our religion teaches that we are the best hominid prototype with the greatest propensity for knowledge and wisdom. In other words, *we* and *we only* were created in the image and likeness of God?'

Oh dear, cosmic racism (or should I say speciesism, since that is the term in current use among many of those who are working towards an acknowledgement of the equality of *all* Gaia's children) rears its ugly head. But let us leave for the moment the world of Paschats and Crystal people and, in fact, any other advanced life form they may have mentioned such as the Dolphin people, and the Lizard people of Auriga and see what our own academics have to say. I have collected a few extracts from *The Encyclopedia of Space Travel and Astronomy,* from the writings of Ian Ridpath and from *Cosmos* by Carl Sagan. The page references are given in the footnotes.

'The possibility that other life-forms may exist in the universe and that we may one day contact them – has been a staple of science fiction novels for a century, or more. Now, however, the subject has moved out of the realms of fiction.'[1]

'The factors in the Drake Equation* *[a formula for estimating the existence of intelligent extraterrestrial life based upon seven variable factors, developed by Frank Drake, of Cornell University]* governing the evolution of intelligence and technology are difficult to assess because we have only the example of ourselves to go on. Anthropologists can trace the dawn of man to three or four million years ago on the plains of Africa. Then, several species of ape-man lived side by side, but only one species survived to become man...

'We are very recent arrivals in the history of the Earth, the product of a long and complex evolutionary chain. It seems inconceivable that the same evolutionary path could be duplicated exactly everywhere else, so how can we hope to find anyone in space remotely resembling ourselves? Fortunately, evolution has the knack of reaching the same result by several different pathways. For instance, several different types of creature have independently invented flight: insects, mammals, reptiles, and even fish. There seem to be good reasons to suppose that intelligent, technological

1 *The Encyclopedia of Space and Astronomy,* Ed. Ian Ridpath, p.99.

beings similar to ourselves have arisen on many planets around our solartype stars throughout the galaxy.

'Of course, local conditions will impose certain differences. On a high-gravity planet, for example, creatures (if they had muscles and bones like ours) are likely to be squat and heavy; whereas on a low gravity planet the beings might be tall and slender, with large noses to breathe the thin air. On planets with vast expanses of flat land, some creatures may have developed wheels rather than legs. If the planet is cold, they could be hairy, and possibly white like polar bears. Some aliens may even look like centaurs, with four legs and two arms.'[1]

* 'The Drake Equation: $N = N_x f p n_e f l f i f_c f L$. All the f's.are fractions, having values between 0 and 1; they will pare down the large value of N.

N_x, the number of stars in the Milky Way Galaxy;
fp, the fraction of stars that have planetary systems;
n_e, the number of planets in a given system that are ecologically suitable for life;
fl, the fraction of otherwise suitable planets on which life actually arises;
f, the fraction of inhabited planets on which an intelligent form of life evolves;
f_c, the fraction of planets inhabited by intelligent beings on which a communicative technical civilization develops;
and
ft, the fraction of a planetary lifetime graced by a technical civilization.

'To derive N we must estimate each of these quantities. We know a fair amount about the early factors in the equation, the number of stars and planetary systems. We know very little about the later factors, concerning the evolution of intelligence or the lifetime of technical societies. In these cases our estimates will be little better than guesses ... One of the great virtues of this equation ... is that it involves subjects ranging from stellar and planetary astronomy to organic chemistry, evolutionary biology, history, politics and abnormal psychology. Much of the Cosmos is in the span of the Drake equation.

---

1 *The Encyclopedia of Space and Astronomy,* Ed. Ian Ridpath, pp.104-105

'We know N, the number of stars in the Milky Way Galaxy, fairly well, by careful counts of stars in small but representative regions of the sky ... some recent estimates place it at 4×10^{11}. Very few of these stars are of the massive short-lived variety that squander their reserves of thermonuclear fuel. The great majority have lifetimes of billions or more years in which they are shining stably, providing a suitable energy source for the origin and evolution of life on nearby planets.

'There is evidence that planets are a frequent accompaniment of star formation: in the satellite systems of Jupiter, Saturn and Uranus, which are like miniature solar systems, in theories of the origin of the planets, in studies of double stars, in observations of accretion disks around stars; and in some preliminary investigations of gravitational perturbations of nearby stars. Many, perhaps, even most, stars may have planets ...'[1]

To go through the entire Drake equation would take far too much time for it is quite complicated, but the most pessimistic estimate is that N equals 1 – our own planet Earth. According to the model given in Professor Sagan's book, however, 'the number of extant civilizations in the galaxy is in the *millions*.' As Sagan points out, however, the real probability is not based so much upon the possible unreliability of our ability to estimate the variables of the Drake equation 'which involve astronomy, organic chemistry, and evolutionary biology, the principal uncertainty comes down to economics and politics and what, on Earth, we call human nature.' He goes on to say: 'It seems fairly clear that if self-destruction is not the overwhelmingly preponderant fate of galactic civilizations, then the sky is softly humming with messages from the stars.'

Sagan makes many more cogent points which I feel are worth quoting as he is one of our world's leading authorities on the subject. I see in these comments much evidence to support, the Paschat and Crystal information and teachings, both in *The Lion People* and this, its sequel.

'I think that life forms on many worlds will consist, by and large, of the same atoms we have here, perhaps even many of the same basic molecules, such as proteins and nucleic acids – but put together in unfamiliar ways. Perhaps

1 *Cosmos*, Carl Sagan, p. 299.

144

organisms that float in dense planetary atmospheres will be very much like us in their atomic composition, except they might not have bones and therefore not need much calcium. Perhaps elsewhere some solvent other than water is used. Hydrofluoric acid might serve rather well, although there is not a great deal of fluorine in the Cosmos; hydrofluoric acid would do a great deal of damage to the kind of molecules that make us up, but other organic molecules, paraffin waxes, for example, are perfectly stable in its presence. Liquid ammonia would make an even better solvent system because ammonia is very abundant in the Cosmos. But it is liquid only on worlds much colder than Earth or Mars. Ammonia is ordinarily a gas on Earth, as water is on Venus. Or perhaps there are living things that do not have a solvent system at all – solid-state life, where there are electrical signals propagating rather than molecules floating about.'[1]

'Were the Earth to be started all over again with all its physical features identical, it is extremely unlikely that anything closely resembling a human being would ever again emerge. There is a powerful random character to the evolutionary process. A cosmic ray striking a different gene, producing a different mutation, can have small consequences early but profound consequences later. Happenstance may play a powerful role in biology, as it does in history. The farther back the critical events occur, the more powerfully can they influence the present.

'For example, consider our hands. We have five fingers, including one opposable thumb. They serve us quite well. But I think we would be served equally well with six fingers including a thumb, or four fingers including a thumb, or maybe five fingers and two thumbs. There is nothing intrinsically best about our particular configuration of fingers, which we ordinarily think of as so natural and inevitable. We have five fingers because we have descended from a Devonian fish that had five phalanges or bones in its fins. Had we descended from a fish with four or six phalanges, we would have four or six fingers on each hand and would think them perfectly natural. We use base ten arithmetic only because we have ten fingers on our hands. Had the arrangement been otherwise, we would use base eight or base twelve arithmetic and relegate

1 *Cosmos,* Carl Sagan, p. 128

base ten to the New Math. The same point applies, I believe, to many more essential aspects of our being – our hereditary material, our internal biochemistry, our form, stature, organ systems,. loves and hates, passions and despairs, tenderness and aggression, even our analytical processes – all of these are, at least in part, the result of apparently minor accidents in our immensely long evolutionary history. Perhaps if one less dragonfly had drowned in the Carboniferous swamps, the intelligent organisms on our planet today would have feathers and teach their young in rookeries. The pattern of evolutionary causality is a web of astonishing complexity; the incompleteness of our understanding humbles us.'[1]

This masterful piece of conjecture certainly begs for more metaphysical comment than I am qualified to give, so I am going to hand over to the Crystal people at this point:

THE CRYSTAL PEOPLE:

Let us take our learned friend up on a few points. The random or chaotic nature of the evolutionary process only *appears* so in its early stages and, although the popular chaos science avows that something as seemingly insignificant as the flutter of a butterfly's wings can alter a future chain of events, one should never lose sight of the fact that the butterfly, as part of the creative process, may be the agent of a much higher power. In other words evolution is inevitably chaotic in its youth, but progresses slowly to order as the desired effects of the original blueprint begin to take shape. Rule of the cosmos: *there is no action that is not preceded by thought.* And where there is thought there is intelligence and where there is intelligence there is a grand design or blueprint.

Where we do concur with Professor Sagan is in his statement that 'a cosmic ray striking a different gene, producing a different mutation, can have small consequences early but profound consequences later'. This is precisely what has happened on your planet as far as the cosmic virus is concerned. At first its effects were concentrated on a small area and a few people, but it has nowspread world-wide and therein lies the problem that the creative forces of light, together with the true ruling essence of your planet, are being obliged to deal with somewhat drastically.

---

1 *Cosmos*, Carl Sagan, p. 282.

Now let us consider the fingers-hands paragraph in Professor Sagan's wise and eloquent thesis; to quote from *THE LION PEOPLE*: 'Our race evolved from a specific cosmic impulse which produces a particular evolutionary strain or genotype. This primary impulse formulated the genetic code that shaped us into the species we ultimately became.'[1] He is also correct in assuming that physical conditions affect the height, shape, even the intelligence factors involved in any evolutionary stream. But there is always the overshadowing influence of the creator; and we do not mean the deity you call God, but the creative force as we have explained it in Chapter 9. The creation *always* reflects the nature of the creator, which does not mean, of course, that because you, as the dominant species on Earth, are of the hominid type, God is also that way and you are therefore in some way privileged above your cosmic relations. It merely means that the intelligences that drew up the blueprint for the evolution of this planet carried a basically hominid impulse and, therefore, hominids were destined to assume the dominant role thereon. However, in other parts of the cosmos, as Professor Sagan has suggested, the species dominating may be and are in fact very different indeed. Among the myriad manifestations of the creative-evolutionary principle, there are physical beings who, although totally dissimilar to yourselves in appearance are, in fact, light years ahead of you in technical and scientific knowledge and spiritual understanding. They may not resemble *your* idea of God; and yet they may be and in many cases are much nearer to the true creative source than any of your kind.

The comment offered by our learned friend on the subject of base ten arithmetic is also interesting. As we and our leonine cousins have explained, there are planets inhabited by beings who function on entirely different numerical systems from your own (see Chapter 2). Such manifestations of matter at any given frequency are built into the original blueprint and their somatic development proceeds accordingly. There are, actually, planets supporting an advanced form of intelligent life that is winged and does, in fact, live in nests, although these habitats are far removed from the nests built by your own birds and, when your bird-life has reached the end of its evolutionary cycle on Earth, the essence-fragments of those feathered beings will be reborn into such a world, wherein they will take their next step up the evolutionary ladder of consciousness.

---

1 *The Lion People*, p. 8.

There are also worlds, albeit of a different frequency and in a universe parallel to your own, where centaurs and satyrs live; and you might be interested to learn that it is to those worlds that certain advanced beings of light are sent to further their cosmic education. This knowledge, which was possessed by the Atlanteans, later filtered through to Greek mythology, appearing in the tales of fabulous beasts who were 'tutors to the gods'.

Thank you, Crystal people. Now for some more comments by Professor Sagan:

'The disaster, whatever it was, that cleared the dinosaurs from the world stage removed the pressure on the mammals. Our ancestors no longer had to live in the shadow of voracious reptiles. We diversified exuberantly and flourished. Twenty million years ago, our immediate ancestors probably still lived in the trees, later descending because the forests receded during a major ice age and were replaced by grassy savannahs. It is not much good to be supremely adapted to life in the trees if there are very few trees. Many arboreal primates must have vanished with the forests. A few eked out a precarious existence on the ground and survived. And one of those lines evolved to become us. No one knows the cause of that climatic change. It may have been a small variation in the intrinsic luminosity of the Sun or in the orbit of the Earth; or massive volcanic eruptions injecting fine dust into the stratosphere, reflecting more sunlight back into space and cooling the Earth. It may have been due to changes in the general circulation of the oceans. Or perhaps the passage of the Sun through a galactic dust cloud. Whatever the cause, we see again how tied our existence is to random astronomical and geological events.

'After we came down from the trees we evolved an upright posture; our hands were free; we possessed excellent binocular vision – we had acquired many of the preconditions for making tools. There was now a real advantage in possessing a large brain and in communicating complex thoughts. Other things being equal, it is better to be smart than to be stupid. Intelligent beings can solve problems better, live longer and leave more offspring; until the invention of nuclear weapons, intelligence powerfully aided survival. In our history it was some horde of furry little mammals who hid from the dinosaurs, colonized the treetops and later scampered down to domesticate fire, invent writing, construct observatories and launch space vehicles. If things had been a little different, it might have been some other creature whose intelligence and manipulative ability would have led to comparable accomplishments. Perhaps the smart bipedal dinosaurs, or the racoons, or the otters, or the squid. It would be nice to know how different other intelligences can be; so we study the whales and the great apes. To learn a little about what other kinds of civilizations are possible, we can study history and cultural anthropology. But we are all of us – us whales, us apes, us people – too closely related. As long as our inquiries are limited to one or two evolutionary lines on a single planet, we will remain forever ignorant of the possible range and brilliance of other intelligences and other civilizations.

'On another planet, with a different sequence of random processes to make hereditary diversity and a different environment to select particular combinations of genes, the chances of finding beings who are physically very similar to us are, I believe, near zero. The chances of finding another form of intelligence are not. Their brains may well have evolved from the inside out. They may have switching elements analagous to our neurons. But the neurons may be very different; perhaps superconductors that work at very low temperatures rather than organic devices that work at room temperature, in which case the speed of thought could be 10^7 times faster than ours. Or perhaps the equivalent of neurons elsewhere would not be in direct physical contact but in radio communication so that a single intelligent being could be distributed among many different organisms, or even many different planets, each with a part of the intelligence of the whole, each contributing by radio to an intelligence much greater than itself. There may be planets where the intelligent beings have about 10^{14} neural connections, as we do. But there may be places where the number is 10^{24} or 10^{34}. I wonder what they would know. Because we inhabit the same universe as they, we and they must share some substantial information in common. If we could make contact, there is much in their brains that would be of great interest to ours. But the opposite is also true. I think extraterrestrial intelligence – even beings substantially further evolved than we – will be interested in us, in what we know, how we think, what our brains are like, the course of our evolution, the prospects for our future.'[1]

This time it is Kaini's turn to comment.

KAINI:

'But, my dear Professor, there *are* single intelligent beings, we call them essences, distributed among different planets and organisms and all experiencing *simultaneously*. But then you would know, would you not (albeit subconsciously), since you are one of 'them'. And, when it comes to inhabiting the same universe, let us not limit that to those spheres you perceive when you consult your telescopes, or resort to your mathematical calculations and equations relating to the physical worlds with which you are most familiar. But rather extend your consciousness to those essence-fragments of yourself that are existing in universes way beyond your physical perception or present computations; and therein you will find the answers to many, if not all, of the questions you pose in this well thought-out (or should I say "remembered"?) thesis.'

What more can I add!

Thank you, Kaini.

THE CLOSE GENETIC RELATIONSHIP BETWEEN *HOMO SAPIENS* AND CHIMPANZEES:

Recent studies of genetic finger-printing have added new dimensions to our understanding of our relationship with the animals with which we shared this planet, the anthropological implications being dramatic. It has now been established that the human, chimp and gorilla all share a common ancestor as recently as five million years ago. Humans, it seems, are more closely akin to the chimpanzees than either humans or chimps are to the gorilla. Only one per cent of our DNA differs from that of the chimps. Certain anthropologists, notably Morris Goodman of Wayne State University, have therefore proposed that humans, chimps

1 Sagan, *op. cit.*, pp. 283-285

and gorillas should now be placed in the same new sub-family, *Homininnae,* instead of leaving humans in proud isolation in their own classification.

One of America's leading ecologists, Professor Jared Diamond of the University of California, however, takes things a step further in suggesting that there are two recognized members of the chimpanzee family, the common chimp and the pigmy chimp. These two chimps being more closely related to humans than either type of chimp, or humans, is to anything else, including the gorilla, logic therefore dictates the correct classification would put the three types of chimpanzee – common, pygmy and human – together in one group, contrasted with the gorillas. Professor Diamond's latest book, *The Rise and Fall of the Third Chimpanzee,* is even more outspoken on these subjects and any reader who would like to know more about his researches and resulting conclusions is referred to the bibliography.

Perhaps the aforegoing may serve to convince the more sceptical among our readers that the Paschat and Crystal people contacts are not as close to the lunatic fringe as might be imagined at first glance. But then today's science fiction is inevitably tomorrow's science and, taking into account the fact that I am by no means the perfect instrument for these revelations, plus the normal human error factor, at least some small percentage of the information will be proven correct. And, if observations effected since the Paschats first entered my humble scenario are correct, that percentage could be quite high! Where-upon I rest my case and leave my readers in the competent hands (and minds!) of my enlightened and loving communicators.

BIBLIOGRAPHY

Budge, E. A. Wallis. *The Gods of The Egyptians, Vols. I & II*
Dover Publications Inc., New York, 1969.

Cleary, Thomas (trans). *Immortal Sisters*
Element/Shambhala, Boston & Shaftesbury, 1989.

Diamond, Jared. *The Rise and Fall of The Third Chimpanzee*
Radius Books, California, USA.

Holroyd, Stuart. *Alien Intelligence*
Abacus Books, London, 1980.

Hope, Murry. *Olympus*
Aquarian / Harper Collins, London, 1991.

Hope, Murry. *Time: The Ultimate Energy*
Element Books Ltd., Shaftesbury, 1991.

Hope, Murry. *Atlantis: Myth or Reality?*
Arkana/Penguin, London, 1991.

Hope, Murry. *Practical Atlantean Magic*
Aquarian/Harper Collins, London, 1992.

Hope, Murry. *The Greek Tradition*
Element Books Ltd., Shaftesbury, 1989.

Hoyle, Fred. *The Intelligent Universe*
Michael Joseph, London, 1983.

Ridpath, Ian (Ed.) *Encyclopedia of Space and Astronomy*
Octopus Books Ltd., London, 1979.

Sagan, Carl. *Cosmos*
Random House, New York, NY, 1981.

Warlow, Peter. *The Reversing Earth*
J. M. Dent & Sons, London, 1982.

White, John. *Pole Shifts*
A.R.E. Press, Virginia Beach, Virginia, U.S.A.

Wolf, Fred Alan. *Parallel Universes*
Bodley Head Ltd., London, 1988.

Also from THOTH PUBLICATIONS:

THE LION PEOPLE

Murry Hope, author of eight books and one of the leading writers on the metaphysics and parapsychology of ancient beliefs, reveals her telepathic communications with the PASCHATS, a race of leonine beings from another world and another time.

DISCOVER:
- **How all life relates to the Central Creative Force.**
- **The reality of other intelligent forms in the universe.**
- **The nature of death, karma and reincarnation.**
- **Why some people seem to have an easy life while others suffer.**
- **How to make time your friend not your enemy.**
- **A new concept of good and evil.**
- **Procedures of healing and self-healing.**
- **New and intriguing ways of self-discovery.**
- **The cosmic connection between Sirius and the planet Earth.**

The author also provides evidence from historical sources, ancient arcane traditions, art, anthropology and astronomy which lend credence to the existence of PASCHATS and support for their message.

If you feel an affinity with felines you will love *THE LION PEOPLE*, a fascinating and gripping revelation from Outer Space and Outer Time.

They are watching, guiding and caring!

ISBN 978 1 870450 01 0

THE GAIA DIALOGUES

Have you ever held a conversation with the spirit of the planet upon which you live, heard her side of the story; her anger at the abuse of her body, and her feelings concerning that errant race we call humanity, large numbers of which she intends to jettison during the Pole Shift that will be precipitated by her approaching quantum leap? Hear it straight from Gaia herself as she tells all in a series of dialogues with fellow alien Murry Hope of *LION PEOPLE* fame!

Read it if you dare – it shocks – it frightens – it defies all conventional esoteric, religious and scientific thinking!

ISBN 978 1870450 18 8